Lecture Notes in Economics and Mathematical Systems

Managing Editors: M. Beckmann and W. Krelle

343

Carl Chiarella

The Elements of a Nonlinear Theory of Economic Dynamics

Springer-Verlag

Berlin Heidelberg New York London Paris Tokyo Hong Kong

Managing Editors

Prof. Dr. M. Beckmann
Brown University
Providence, RI 02912, USA

Prof. Dr. W. Krelle
Institut für Gesellschafts- und Wirtschaftswissenschaften
der Universität Bonn
Adenauerallee 24–42, D-5300 Bonn, FRG

Author

Prof. Carl Chiarella
School of Finance and Economics
University of Technology, Sydney
P.O. Box 123, Broadway 2077 N.S.W., Australia

ISBN 3-540-52622-6 Springer-Verlag Berlin Heidelberg New York
ISBN 0-387-52622-6 Springer-Verlag New York Berlin Heidelberg

Printing and binding: Druckhaus Beltz, Hemsbach/Bergstr.
2142/3140-543210 – Printed on acid-free paper

PREFACE

The aim of this set of notes is to provide a framework for the application of the concepts and techniques of the modern theory of nonlinear dynamical systems to the analysis of models of economic dynamics. The first chapter surveys the need for a nonlinear theory of economic dynamics. Such a need arises not only in analysing endogenous theories of the business cycle, but also from the analysis of a number of dynamic economic models which seem to display perverse stability behaviour. Chapter two surveys the principal results and techniques of the theory of dynamical systems relevant to our applications. Chapter three applies these techniques to view the older endogenous cycle theories in a unified mathematical framework, which more readily allows a qualitative analysis of the economic cycle. In chapter four we analyse the locally unstable equilibrium of a macroeconomic model incorporating the government budget constraint and show that the model can exhibit stable limit cycle motion. In chapter five we show how centre manifold concepts may be applied to analyse a three dimensional dynamic economic model which is a simple extension of Goodwin's model of the dynamic interaction of workers and capitalists and which displays limit cycle behaviour. In chapter six we analyse a discrete time version of the classical cobweb model and show that the introduction of a simple nonlinearity can cause the model to exhibit that bounded, recurrent but nonperiodic motion known as chaos. In chapter seven we analyse from an entirely new point of view the dynamic instability problem which arises in a large number of perfect foresight and rational expectations models of interest in many areas of economic analysis. We take as the paradigmatic example of such behaviour one of the basic perfect foresight models of monetary dynamics and show that once appropriate nonlinearities are introduced and additional equilibrium concepts such as limit cycles and chaotic motion are admitted the "problem" may be resolved. In the final chapter we indicate a number of problems in the areas of economic dynamics which we believe could be seen in a new light if analysed with the techniques and concepts that we have applied in these notes.

After remaining in the wings of the economic stage for many years the nonlinear approach to dynamic analysis now seems to be moving towards centre-stage, judging from the large number of books and articles which have appeared in recent years. Other works which could be read in conjunction with this one include Medio (1979), Gabisch and Lorenz (1989), Lorenz (1989) and Ferri and Greenberg (1989).

This set of notes grew out of a thesis submitted to the University of New South Wales and is the result of my musings over several years on certain aspects of economic dynamics. Consequently I owe a debt to a number of people who, wittingly or unwittingly and for good or ill, have influenced the development of my thinking about economic theory.

Firstly I wish to thank my thesis supervisor Professor M.C. Kemp for encouraging, stimulating and guiding my interest in a wide range of areas in mathematical economics and for willingly allowing me to submit a thesis which is quite different to the one which we, and certainly he, had originally anticipated.

I owe a particular intellectual debt to Professor J.M. Blatt (formerly of the University of New South Wales) whose criticism of the economic theorist's heavy reliance on linear models in both his published work and at a number of seminars in the Economics Theory Workshop at the University of New South Wales has had an obvious influence on my thinking. Indeed it was whilst attending a joint seminar of the Economic Society of N.S.W. and the Australian Mathematical Society in 1977, at which Professor Blatt presented what became the first of his series of articles in Oxford Economic Papers, that I originally conceived the idea of a systematic study of economic dynamics via the methods of the theory of nonlinear dynamical systems.

I have benefitted from discussions with a number of people on various aspects of the work reported here. In particular I would like to thank the late Professor Richard Manning (SUNY, Buffalo), Professor Daniel Leonard (University of New South Wales) and Chris Boyd (Universite Catholique de Louvain, Belgium). I am indebted to Professor Hans-Walter Lorenz (Georg-August-Universitat Gottingen) for having taken the trouble to read through an early draft of these notes and having made a number of valuable suggestions.

I am also indebted to Professors Alfred Steinherr and Daniel Weiserbs of IRES, l'Univesite Catholique de Louvain for making possible my two visits to that institution. The stimulating research environment which I enjoyed there has had a decisive influence on the development of this work.

None of the above mentioned persons should be held responsible for any misconceptions and shortcomings that may appear in these notes.

v

Finally I would like to thank my wife, Lyn, and children, Claudine and Adrian, for tolerating the long hours I spent in my study and for providing such an ideal home environment.

The University of Technology, Sydney

January 1990

CONTENTS

CHAPTER 1. **THE NEED FOR A NONLINEAR THEORY OF ECONOMIC DYNAMICS**

1.1 **Introduction**

The inter-war years produced some of the richest theories in the history of economic
thought and it was for this reason that Shackle (1967) entitled his now classical
work on theoretical developments in that era "The Years of High Theory". The period
saw in particular the development of the theories of Hayek, Keynes, Harrod, Kalecki,
The Stockholm School and Schumpeter which aimed at explaining various aspects of the
dynamic evolution of the capitalist economy. The 1930s culminated with Samuelson's
"Foundations of Economic Analysis", even though this work was not published until
1947. The original 1941 version carried the subtitle "The Operational Significance
of Economic Theory" and was a major landmark in theoretical economic analysis as it
provided a framework in which the particular problems and viewpoints of the earlier
mentioned theorists could be handled in a unified general way.

In particular Samuelson systematized the comparative static mode of analysis. The
basic idea of this type of analysis is to express the relationships of the model of
the economic system under investigation in terms of a set of algebraic equations
whose solution represents the equilibrium of the system. Such models generally
involve a set of parameters and the object of comparative static analysis is to
determine how the equilibrium points are affected by changes in the parameters. This
is achieved by linearizing the algebraic equations around the equilibrium and then
using the techniques of matrix algebra to determine the position of the new
equilibrium and its dependence on parametric changes. In this setting the question
of economic dynamics arises when one asks whether the economic system will actually
approach the new equilibrium. This question is answered by use of the concepts of
point stability and instability from the theory of linear dynamical systems. In such
analyses the economic theorist is only interested in stable equilibrium points;
unstable equilibria are generally ruled out by invoking Samuelson's correspondence
principle. This principle uses the postulate of stability to determine the sign of
determinants which are crucial in the comparison of static equilibria.

In mathematical terms the comparative static framework tacitly assumes that the only
type of relevant equilibria are points in n-dimensional space (n being the dimension
of the economic model under consideration) and the only relevant dynamic behaviour is
governed by local linearisation around the equilibrium. The resulting *linear*
dynamical system involves paths approaching this equilibrium either monotonically or
in damped oscillatory fashion. The main mathematical tool of this dynamic analysis

is the theory of linear difference or ordinary differential equations. Point equilibria are the only type of equilibria that such equations can exhibit, apart possibly from a family of periodic solutions whose amplitudes depend upon the initial conditions. These periodic solutions can occur only for a particular set of parameter values and are lost when the parameters of the model are given an *arbitrary* change; in mathematical parlance these solutions are said to be structurally unstable. In two dimensional models governed by differential equations these periodic solutions correspond to the case when the Jacobian matrix of the system has pure complex eigenvalues.

The use of comparative statics in conjunction with linear stability theory to analyse dynamic behaviour has recently attracted criticism from Blatt (1983) and Kregel (1980). However the approach is not to be totally decried as it has enabled the economic theorist to construct an impressive body of theory, e.g. optimizing behaviour of various kinds, international trade theory, traditional macroeconomic theory. However it is the contention of this thesis that there are a number of important issues in dynamic economic theory which cannot be properly addressed with the foregoing mode of analysis and indeed use of that analysis may, and does, lead to some serious misconceptions.

In recent years much criticism has been levelled at the very concept of equilibrium not only as expressed in the comparative static mode of analysis but more generally in the standard neoclassical framework. One particularly cogent criticism is that of Kaldor (1972) who attacks the axiomatic nature of general equilibrium theory. Of relevance to our discussion however is Kaldor's criticism that the standard equilibrium notion carries the assumption '...that the operation of economic forces is constrained by a set of exogenous variables which are "given" from the outside and stable over time'. The economic system is seen as operating in such a way that it will converge to a *unique point* whose characteristics are determined by the static exogenous variables. Kaldor saw this scheme as an unsatisfactory basis for a theory of economic dynamics, as continuous economic change could only come about through some kind of moving equilibrium presumably as a result of time changes in the exogenous variables occuring in such a way as to be consistent with continuous equilibrium through time. Kaldor believed that a proper theory of economic dynamics would have economic change occuring *endogenously*. Kaldor goes on to discuss a far broader range of issues than those we have just cited but from the perspective of the limited terms of reference of this thesis the cited remarks give support to the need for a broader range of equilibrium concepts which can accommodate endogenous economic change.

Blatt's (1983) criticism of the standard equilibrium concept is similar in spirit to that of Kaldor, simply pointing out that the theory of economic dynamics based on the moving equilibrium concept does not square at all with a century and half of experience in decentralised economies which is one of recurrent oscillations in the level of economic activity.

Whilst dynamic economic theory based on linear stability theory has been dominant in recent decades and has led economists to concentrate almost exclusively on the comparative static aspects of economic theory there has nevertheless been a strong and continuing theory of economic dynamics which does not in all situations consider the static equilibrium as a likely or desirable outcome for many economic systems. Many of the dynamic theories formulated during the "years of high theory", particularly those of Hayek, Harrod, Kaldor, the Stockholm school and Schumpeter were examples of what the mathematician would now call self-sustaining oscillations and these cannot be discussed with the comparative static mode of analysis. Nonlinear stability theory is required to analyse such phenomena and in the decade following the appearance of Samuelson's Foundations, when the modes of analysis which still dominate macroeconomic theorizing were formed, the techniques of nonlinear stability theory were still not well developed and were widely known only to those familiar with the specialized literature of electric circuit theory. So of all of the earlier mentioned pre-war theories it is perhaps not surprising that the Keynesian system came to dominate as much of its major message is readily expressed in the language of comparative statics. The other more inherently dynamic theories were not so readily if at all expressed in succinct mathematical forms. Kregel (1980) points out that as a result many of the interesting innovations that surfaced in the 1930s were eliminated from subsequent discussion and analysis. The task of comparing the theories of the inter-war years within a unified framework still lies ahead as it requires a truly dynamic mode of analysis.

1.2 **Early Nonlinear Theories**

The post-war years saw an increasing pace in the mathematisation of economic arguments with the Arrow-Debreu general equilibrium scheme in a more or less abstract form dominating the mode of analysis. To the general practitioner economic theorist the stock-in-trade became the comparative static mode of analysis with its implicit assumption that only locally stable point equilibria were worthy of study.

A theoretical underpinning of the local stability assumptions was the Frisch (1933) view of the business cycle which came to dominate in the post-war years. According to this view the economy is stable but is prevented from attaining its equilibrium point because of exogenous shocks which impinge upon the system. The mathematical expression of this concept is a set of stable linear differential or difference equations with stochastic terms appended to the right hand side. Econometric evidence, particularly that of Hickman (1972), seemed to confirm this view and so the comparative static analysis of locally stable equilibrium points became the dominant mode of thought. Recently Blatt (1978, 1980, 1983) has challenged the evidence in favour of stable linear models of the business cycle and urges the use of nonlinear models. The present thesis is in part an attempt to answer that call.

There were nevertheless a number of early attempts to mathematise the dynamic economic theories of the pre-war era using locally unstable nonlinear models. In particular the work of Kaldor (1940), Hicks (1950), Goodwin (1950, 1951 and 1967) and Allais (1956). In these works the nonlinearities and time lags inherent in the models considered generate persistent economic fluctuations. Many of these early nonlinear theories were brilliant in conception as their authors relied on an intuitive understanding of the problem at hand to construct the required model. At the time the techniques of nonlinear differential equations were neither sufficiently developed nor widely known to make the construction of these early nonlinear theories a routine matter. As we shall see in chapter three, with our knowledge of the modern theory of dynamical systems this is now possible. The fact that the construction of nonlinear models could not be reduced to the routine application of certain mathematical techniques probably also contributed to the dominance of the comparative static-locally stable type of models, which could be so reduced.

Recent years have started to see a trickle of books and articles on nonlinear models employing some of the modern mathematical theories. The book by Medio (1979) systematizes the early theories of Kaldor, Hicks and Goodwin. Chang and Smyth (1971), Schinasi (1981, 1982) and Torre (1977) apply various concepts from the modern theory of dynamical systems to analyse nonlinear models.

Before concluding this section it is perhaps appropriate to dispel any illusion that we may have created that the overconcentration on comparative static methods is somehow due to Samuelson's Foundations. Certainly the Foundations cemented and routinized the role of comparative statics in economic theory. However in the penultimate chapter entitled "Some Fundamentals of Dynamical Theory" Samuelson outlines several approaches to dynamic economic theory and certainly discusses the use of nonlinear models, quoting as an example the Van der Pol equation which is the classic paradigm of self-sustaining oscillations in two dimensions and is at the base of most of the nonlinear theories mentioned earlier. This chapter of Samuelson still makes worthwhile reading and to the knowledge of this writer his ideas on nonlinear stochastic systems have still not been developed.

1.3 Development of the Theory of Dynamical Systems

Progress in any scientific discipline is very much a function of the mathematical concepts and tools which are at hand to forge and articulate the paradigm models which are an essential part of scientific understanding. This process forms a feedback mechanism since mathematical progress in its turn is often a function of the scientific problems of the time. The best example of this interaction is the development of classical mechanics from the time of Newton and then quantum mechanics from the early decades of the present century. Therefore to understand the development of a scientific discipline it is important to not only understand the development of the paradigms of the discipline but also the development of the mathematical ideas which are interacting with these paradigms.

To understand the course of the past development of the theory of economic dynamics as well as to see why we have entered an era when new approaches are possible it is well worthwhile outlining briefly the broad history of the evolution of the theory of dynamical systems.

The origins of the subject lie in the experimental work of Galileo and Kepler on the motion of earth bound objects and of the planetary system. The mathematical theory of dynamical systems starts with Newton who pulled together a unified theory of planetary motion from the physical concepts of Galileo and Kepler and the embryonic notions of the calculus with which mathematicians had been grappling for the previous century. Interestingly enough from the point of view of later developments Newton's approach to dynamical systems was largely geometric. The presentation of the theory of dynamical systems which comes down to us originates with Leibniz's development of the calculus. His development was in a clear and easy to use notation (which is why it is still in use three centuries later) and led calculus along the path of symbolic/analytic techniques which were greatly developed by Euler (1707-1783). The stage was thus set for Lagrange (1736-1813) who wrote a definitive and influential text on planetary motion using and extending the analytical techniques of Euler ; it is alleged by some writers that Lagrange boasted about the fact that his text did not contain a single diagram.

The basic aim of the symbolic/analytic approach to the theory of dynamical systems was to express the solution of the governing differential or difference equations in terms of known functions (such as trigonometric or exponential) or if this could not be done and the differential equation were of sufficient interest then to define a new "special" function, usually in terms of an infinite series - e.g. Bessel and Legendre functions. This approach has been dubbed classical by Abraham and Shaw

(1984) and a number of other modern writers and its essence was to obtain a
quantitative solution.

The classical period of the theory of dynamical systems started to attain its
culmination towards the end of the nineteenth century, by which time most of the
problems which yielded easily to this approach had been solved and it was realised
that the technique did not carry over to an investigation of a number of nonlinear
dynamical systems which were being encountered.

The new approach was set by Poincaré (1854-1912) who revived the earlier geometric
concepts of Newton. Poincaré emphasized the qualitative, global aspects of solutions
of dynamical systems in phase space. It is of interest to note that the economic
theorist's use of arrow diagrams in dynamic analysis is inspired by this general
approach and makes economics one of the scientific disciplines in which these
techniques started to have wide use. Another important contributor to the
development of the qualitative geometric viewpoint was Liapunov (1857-1918) who
developed the basic concepts of stability.

During the development of the qualitative theory the issues which have led to much
progress are the theory of self sustaining oscillations, bifurcation phenomena,
structural stability and chaotic behaviour. Significant contributions to all but the
last of these topics were made by Andronov (1901-1952) and his co-workers and are
reported in his classical work "The Theory of Oscillators" published in the U.S.S.R.
in 1936. The concepts and techniques of this book, with the addition of a few
embellishments from more recent results are quite adequate for the economic theorist
who wishes to analyse nonlinear models of economic dynamics. Certainly most of the
dynamic models that we analyse are inspired by the Andronov approach.

The last mentioned of the above issues, chaotic behaviour, had already surfaced in
the works of Poincaré and Birkhoff (1884-1944). However it was only with the advent
of the high speed digital computer that mathematicians began to realise the
importance of this aspect of dynamic behaviour. The wide-spread availability of easy
to use computer power allowed scientific workers to "solve" the computing problem
posed by dynamical systems, a problem whose solution had stagnated since the golden
age of the classical era. Whilst obtaining computer solutions of a set of three
ordinary differential equations, Lorenz (1963) observed that for certain parameter
ranges solutions tended to a peculiar limit set which has come to be known as a
strange attractor. At about the same time and independently Smale (1963) produced
his famous horseshoe construction which is now one of the classic examples of a
chaotic limit set in the mathematical sense. Progress on chaotic dynamics has been
very rapid since that time. From a type of behaviour of which mathematicians were
almost ignorant it is now realised that for nonlinear differential equations of order

greater than two and for even one-dimensional nonlinear difference equations this type of behaviour is generic i.e. more likely to be the norm.

In chapter two we survey those concepts in the modern qualitative theory of dynamical systems which are relevant to our subsequent discussion of economic dynamics. Our approach is discursive and geometric - we do not attempt to prove any theorems but we do outline some of the basic techniques such as the Hopf bifurcation theorem, the method of averaging, the method of relaxation oscillations and centre manifold expansions.

1.4 Problems in the Current State of Economic Dynamics

The principal aim of this thesis is to routinize nonlinear methods for the analysis of dynamic economic models. The approach we adopt mirrors the comparative static mode of analysis which considers locally stable equilibria and the effect on them of parameter changes; the local stability assumption guarantees that time paths will converge to the new equilibrium. In our nonlinear analysis we consider situations where the equilibrium point becomes locally unstable but it is possible to establish the existence of a stable oscillatory path to which all time paths are tending. The methods we employ allow us to gauge the effect of model parameter changes on the amplitude of the oscillation. The areas to which we have chosen to apply the nonlinear mode of analysis are a number of long-standing models which we felt could particularly benefit from a different viewpoint. We shall now outline those areas and at the same time give a chapter by chapter outline of the thesis.

The need for a nonlinear theory of economic dynamics makes itself felt in many areas of economic analysis but perhaps in none as much as in the theory of the business cycle. Interest in this topic has waxed and waned since the early nineteenth century according to the economic conditions of the times. Certainly there has been a resurgence of interest in recent times as evidenced by the recent surveys of Mullineux (1984) and Zarnowitz (1985). These authors divide business cycle theories into two broad categories. The first concentrates on endogenous factors within the economic system; models of this ilk are driven by changes in investment, credit expansion, the price-cost-profit relationship or the conflict over distributive shares. The existence of time lags and nonlinearities in some of the just mentioned relationships cause the economic system to generate a self-sustaining oscillation which is the business cycle. The mathematical expression of these theories is via deterministic differential or difference equations. The second category concentrates on exogenous factors and are usually associated with economists of the monetarist school. The principal exogenous factors or shocks that set off business fluctuations are government policy actions which have assumed great importance in the post world war two industrialised economies because of the large size of the public sector. The monetarist thesis that changes in the stock of money are the principal cause of changes in real output was also a key influence in the development of the exogenous policy shock theories. The random policy shocks lead to price surprises and miscalculations as economic agents adjust to the surprises via some form of intertemporal substitution. The mathematical expression of these theories is usually in terms of stochastic linear difference equations.

The mode of analysis that we develop in this thesis has evolved with the first category of endogenous theories in mind, since these must involve nonlinear elements in order to generate self sustaining cycles. However they are not without interest to the second category of cycle theories, as, according to evidence cited by Zarnowitz these theories do not provide a satisfactory theory of the business cycle and they may require some additional propagation mechanism such as an investment accelerator.

In chapter three we use the concepts and techniques of chapter two to take a new look at some of the older endogenous cycle theories. The approach adopted reduces the analysis to a study of the limit cycle solutions of nonlinear differential equations in two dimensions.

An area which we also show can benefit from the adoption of a nonlinear viewpoint is the macroeconomic literature on the dynamics of models incorporating the government budget constraint. A characteristic of such models is the appearance of perverse stability results i.e. the stable equilibria display comparative static behaviour which is opposite to what one would expect from traditional macroeconomic theory. In chapter four we approach this class of models by applying some of the nonlinear techniques discussed in chapter two and show that some of the perverse stability results can be reconciled if we allow for the possibility of limit cycle equilibria.

The mathematical expression of the models discussed in chapters three and four is limit cycle motion in the plane with the methods of averaging and relaxation oscillations being the main tools of analysis. In chapter five we see how the economic theorist may escape the confines of the two-dimensional plane by use of centre-manifold theory. There we consider a simple extension of Goodwin's (1967) model of cyclical growth which is expressed as a nonlinear system of three differential equations. The theory of chapter two indicates that the system possesses a limit cycle in three dimensions and we are able to analyse its characteristics.

A standard criticism of limit cycles as models of economic fluctuations is that their dynamic motion is regular and predictable. In the last section of chapter two we indicate that recent developments in the theory of nonlinear dynamics show that nonlinear models can also exhibit irregular and unpredictable oscillatory motion. In chapter six we illustrate this so called chaotic motion on probably the most fundamental paradigm of economic dynamics, namely the cobweb model of price and quantity adjustment in a single (typically agricultural) market. Leontief (1934) gives a fairly complete account of the early theory, however the modern discussion of the dynamic behaviour of this model seems to start with Ezekiel (1938) who first gave the local stability conditions of the model. The subsequent literature is quite extensive and we shall discuss it in chapter six. However the point to stress is that save for one or two exceptions most of this literature is developed within the framework of the comparative static, linear stability theory mode of analysis. The cobweb model is the paradigm par excellence for presenting the bare bones of this mode of analysis which explains its prominence not only in books on economic dynamics such as Gandolfo (1980) but also in texts on mathematical modelling which present it as an example of the use of mathematics in economic analysis, see e.g.Meyer (1984).

For our purposes as well the cobweb model shall serve as the simplest paradigm in which to introduce all of the concept of chaotic motion. However the nonlinear analysis of the cobweb model which we present in chapter six is not only an expository device. Meadows (1970) had already pointed to the need to incorporate nonlinearities and the recent discussion of the cobweb model by Sheffrin (1983) in relation to the rational expectations literature makes this analysis timely and apposite.

One specific area where modern dynamic economic theory seems to be crying out for a nonlinear viewpoint is the class of models displaying the so called dynamic instability problem. This problem refers to the saddle point behaviour in a wide range of descriptive dynamic models and in particular models of monetary dynamics, exchange rate dynamics and macroeconomic models containing markets for homogeneous output, money and bonds. These models all involve some type of expectations mechanisms on returns from financial assets. Whilst saddle point behaviour is a desirable property in dynamic optimising models since it provides a rationale for choosing certain unknown initial values it is a troublesome feature of descriptive dynamic models since all initial values are assumed known. As a result it is necessary to impose arbitrary initial jumps on some of the variables of the model under investigation in order that the ensuing dynamic motion remain on a stable manifold. Whilst the technique just described has become a standard one there nevertheless remain some nagging doubts as to its theoretical basis. Blanchard (1981) in analysing a dynamic model of output, the stock market and interest rates which displays saddle point behaviour describes the technique as "a standard if not entirely convincing practice". There have been various attempts to provide some rationale for the imposition of arbitrary initial jumps; Obstfeld and Rogoff (1983) attempt to provide an encompassing dynamic optimising framework in which the arbitrary initial jumps are imposed by the optimisation procedure; Hadjimichalakis (1981) attempts to get around the problem by explicitly modelling the effect of the opportunity cost of holding money.

All of these attempted solutions to the dynamic instability problem suffer from the defect that they analyse the dynamics within the framework of *linear* differential or difference equations. This framework has the disadvantage of allowing a limited set of equilibrium concepts, namely point equilibria and families of closed cycles which are structurally unstable. We shall show in chapter seven that the adoption of a nonlinear viewpoint and the application of the concepts of limit cycle and chaotic motion enable us to sidestep the dynamic instability problem. This is achieved because it is now possible to have locally unstable equilibrium points without time paths necessarily diverging to infinity.

In chapter eight we take stock of what has been achieved in the preceding chapters and indicate a number of obvious extensions to the models analysed. We also indicate a number of other issues which we believe could benefit from the nonlinear viewpoint. We point out the possibility of some further theoretical developments and the implications of the nonlinear viewpoint for empirical research in economics.

CHAPTER 2   **THE THEORY OF DYNAMICAL SYSTEMS**

2.1 Introduction

Our aim in this chapter is to expound those aspects of the theory of dynamical systems which shall be most relevant to our later investigations. Our approach will be discursive in that we shall try to paint a broad brush picture of the concepts and techniques of the modern qualitative geometric view of the theory of dynamical systems. We have already outlined in chapter one the revolution in the approach to the analysis of dynamical systems which has occured in recent years. Our exposition is inspired by the works of Arnold (1973) and Hirsch and Smale (1974), which were the first texts to diffuse the modern concepts to a broad mathematical audience, and the recent text of Guckenheimer and Holmes (1983), which is a very readable account of some of the most recent developments such as strange attractors and chaotic behaviour. Whilst we do not prove any theorems and our exposition places much emphasis on geometric arguments, as the liberal sprinkling of diagrams will bear witness, our discussion does become a little more technical when we expound two of the major tools of analysis of nonlinear dynamical systems namely the method of averaging and the method of relaxation oscillations.

When it comes to illustrating the concepts and techniques that we discuss we shall break with the tradition of most of the standard texts and use economic examples rather than examples from mechanics and electric circuit theory where much of the modern theory had its origins. As a result we are able to use the modern ideas to present some of the earlier disparate theories of the business cycle within a unified framework. It should be pointed out that a number of authors have already presented various aspects of the theory of dynamical systems from the viewpoint of the economic theorist rather than from that of the physicist or control engineer, in particular the texts of Kemp and Kimura (1978), Gandolfo (1980) and Lorenz (1989).

2.2 Existence and Uniqueness Results

For much of our subsequent discussion we shall be considering dynamical systems which can be expressed in terms of the autonomous differential system

$$\dot{x} = f(x). \qquad (2.1)$$

Here . denotes differentiation with respect to time, x is an n-dimensional vector and f an n-dimensional vector function. In concise mathematical notation we may write $x \in R^n$ and $f: R^n \rightarrow R^n$. Typically we are given some initial value $x(0) \in R^n$. The existence and uniqueness theorems place emphasis on the properties of the solution curve coming out of this initial point. This theory is extremely intricate and technical but is essential as we cannot undertake any study of dynamical systems until we know whether a solution exists and is unique.

The key result in this area is that if in a neighbourhood of the initial point the function f is either differentiable or is continuous and satisfies a Lipschitz condition (which ensures that f does not oscillate too wildly around the initial point), then in a finite time interval existence and uniqueness of the solution is ensured. The Lipschitz condition allows us to deal with cases where f is defined in a piecewise linear fashion and we shall encounter such a case in chapter four. The same conditions also ensure that the solutions vary smoothly as the initial conditions are varied. Thus if $y(t)$ and $z(t)$ are both solutions of equation (2.1) on the closed interval $[t_0, t_1]$ and f has the Lipschitz constant K then for all $t \in [t_0, t_1]$,

$$||y(t) - z(t)|| \leq ||y(t_0) - z(t_0)|| \exp[K(t-t_0)].$$

The existence and continuous dependence concepts are illustrated in figure 2.1 where we see typical solutions originating from the set $||y(t_0) - z(t_0)|| < \delta$. It is important to realize that all of these concepts are *local* and that in particular the continuous dependence result does not preclude the possibility that solutions starting from nearby points separate exponentially rapidly as illustrated in figure 2.2. It is precisely this property which gives chaotic solutions their important characteristics.

A complete characterization of the solutions of arbitrary nonlinear differential equations by either analytic or qualitative methods is impossible and for this reason an extensive theory was developed for linear differential equations and we shall now survey the key aspects of that theory.

2.3   The Linear System $\dot{x} = Ax$

The study of the solutions of the linear system $\dot{x} = Ax$ proceeds via a study of the eigenvalues and eigenvectors of the system matrix A. Considering first the two-dimensional case it is a standard result (see e.g. Hirsch and Smale (1974)) that from the eigenvectors of A we can form a matrix P such that in the new coordinates z

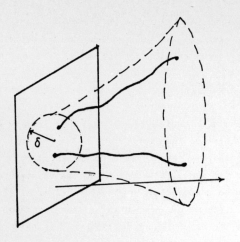 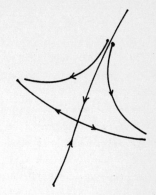

Figure 2.1 Continuous dependence   Figure 2.2 Exponential separation

defined by the transformation z = Px the differential system 2.1 becomes

$$\dot{z} = \begin{bmatrix} \lambda_1 & 0 \\ 0 & \lambda_2 \end{bmatrix} z \ , \tag{2.2}$$

in the case where A has real distinct eigenvalues λ_1 , λ_2 and

$$\dot{z} = \begin{bmatrix} \alpha & \beta \\ -\beta & \alpha \end{bmatrix} z \ , \tag{2.3}$$

in the case when A has complex eigenvalues $\alpha \pm i\beta$. By further transforming to polar coordinates (r,θ) in the z-plane this latter system can be reduced to the simple differential system

$$\dot{r} = \alpha r \quad \text{and} \quad \dot{\theta} = \beta. \tag{2.4}$$

Note that we have dealt neither, with the case when the real eigenvalues are equal nor, with the case when one eigenvalue is zero, as we shall not have occasion to deal with such systems mainly because they are structurally unstable (a term we shall explain later).

In the case of real distinct eigenvalues the solution of (2.2) falls into one of three classifications. If λ_1, λ_2 are both negative then both $z_1(t)$ and $z_2(t)$ are tending exponentially to the origin which in this case is said to be *asymptotically stable*. If λ_1, λ_2 are both positive then $z_1(t)$ and $z_2(t)$ are both moving exponentially away from the origin which is now said to be *asymptotically unstable*. If λ_1, λ_2 are of opposite sign, say $\lambda_1 < 0$ and $\lambda_2 > 0$, then $z_1(t)$ moves exponentially towards the origin while $z_2(t)$ moves exponentially away from the origin which in this case is said to be *saddle-point stable*. Figure 2.3 summarizes each of these cases.

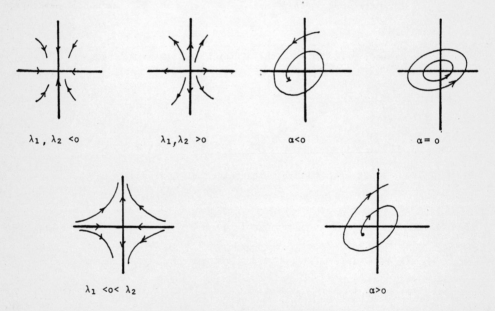

$\lambda_1, \lambda_2 < 0$ $\lambda_1, \lambda_2 > 0$ $\alpha < 0$ $\alpha = 0$

$\lambda_1 < 0 < \lambda_2$ $\alpha > 0$

<u>Figure 2.3</u> Real eigenvalues   <u>Figure 2.4</u> Complex eigenvalues

In the case of complex eigenvalues motion in the z-plane is best understood by considering equation (2.4). Irrespective of the sign of the real part α the polar angle θ is rotating with angular speed β. Thus if $\alpha < 0$ then motion is spiralling towards the origin which is thus asymptotically stable whilst if $\alpha > 0$ then motion is spiralling away from the origin which is then asymptotically unstable. In the border line case $\alpha = 0$, when the eigenvalues are pure complex, solution curves form circles around the origin - solution curves with initial values a distance of r from the origin will always remain the same distance from the origin. In this case the origin is said to be a *centre*. These cases are illustrated in figure 2.4.

The corresponding qualitative picture of solution behaviour in the original x coordinates is obtained by smoothly deforming figures 2.3 and 2.4 since the z_1, z_2 axes correspond to obliquely intersecting lines in the x-plane. If we imagine figures 2.3 and 2.4 to be drawn on sheets of rubber then the corresponding picture in the x-plane can be obtained by pushing and pulling (but *not* tearing) these sheets in various directions. We illustrate a typical such transformation in figure 2.5.

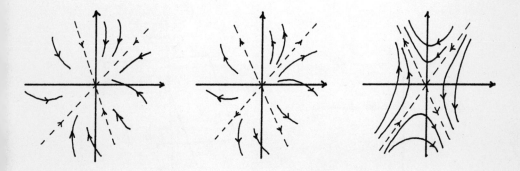

Figure 2.5 Behaviour in the original coordinates

A concept to which we shall occasionally be appealing is that of *structural stability*. A differential system , in the linear case characterised by the matrix A and in the nonlinear case by the function f, is said to be structurally stable if it is possible to find *arbitrary* perturbations to A or f which leave the solutions qualitatively the same. Referring to figures 2.3 and 2.4 the only system which is not structurally stable is the one corresponding to pure complex eigenvalues. Whilst it is certainly true that there exist perturbations to the matrix A which retain the pure complex nature of the eigenvalues these perturbations would not be arbitrary. For similar reasons systems having real and equal eigenvalues are also structurally unstable.

The study of $\dot{x} = Ax$ when $x \in R^n$ can be built up from the two dimensional picture by use of the Jordan canonical form. From the eigenvectors of A it is possible to form the matrix P which via the transformation z=Px reduces the original dynamical system to the form $\dot{z} = Jz$. In the case of distinct eigenvalues the matrix J is block diagonal in structure and may be written $J = \text{diag}(J_+, J_-, J_c)$ where J_+ is a block diagonal matrix consisting of all the positive real part eigenvalues, J_- of all the negative real part eigenvalues and J_c of all the pure complex eigenvalues. This structure allows us to geometrically conceive of the qualitative behaviour in much the same way as we did for the two dimensional system. For instance if there are no pure complex eigenvalues then we could represent the z phase space as shown in figure 2.6 where the axis labelled E_+ is called the unstable manifold (of dimension equal to the number of positive real value eigenvalues) and the axis labelled E_- is called the stable manifold (of dimension equal to the number of negative real value eigenvalues). Essentially we see a kind of generalised n-dimensional saddle point. On this scheme it is best to represent solutions arising from any pure complex eigenvalues as a third manifold E_c perpendicular to E_+ and E_- as shown in figure 2.7. The manifold E_c is known as the *centre manifold*.

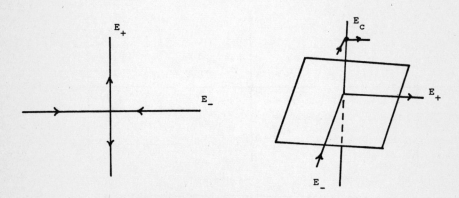

Figure 2.6 Real eigenvalues in R^n Figure 2.7 Complex eigenvalues in R^n

For instance a three dimensional system having a real negative eigenvalue and a pair of pure comlex eigenvalues would have a z phase space as shown in figure 2.8 and the more compact manifold diagram shown in figure 2.9.

In view of what we shall discuss in subsequent sections the important aspect of the solution of n-dimensional linear systems is that they do not introduce any qualitative behaviour which was not present in two dimensional systems. We still have some combination of motion towards the origin, motion away from the origin and families of closed circular orbits around the origin. New qualitative behaviour is introduced when we turn to a study of nonlinear systems. It is for this reason that

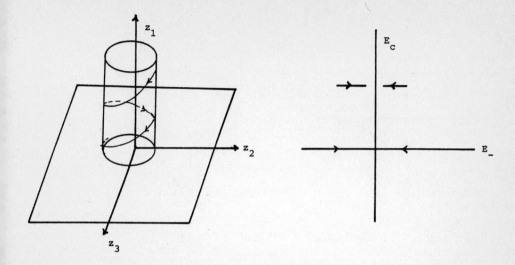

Figure 2.8 A typical 3-dimensional motion   **Figure 2.9** Jordan form $J = \text{diag}(J_-, J_c)$

we must be cautious of basing a theory of economic dynamics exclusively on the concepts of linear dynamical systems as these can exhibit only a subset of the rich dynamical behaviour possible in nonlinear systems.

2.4 Nonlinear Systems on the Plane

The next step in the development of solution concepts comes from a consideration of the nonlinear system

$$\dot{x} = f(x), \qquad\qquad\qquad (2.5)$$

where $x \in R^2$ and $f: R^2 \to R^2$. Because of the nonlinear nature of the function f the system 2.5 may have a number of equilibrium points which are defined as points where $f(x)=0$. This is in contrast to structurally stable linear systems which can only have one equilibrium point, as discussed in section 2.3.

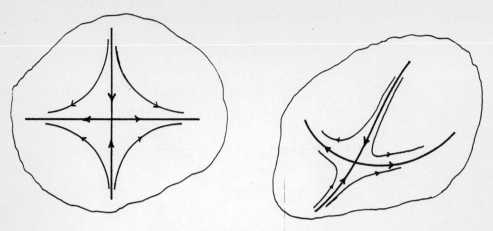

Figure 2.10 Topological equivalence

The qualitative behaviour of the system is determined by first of all performing a local linear analysis around each equilibrium point i.e. around the equilibrium point $\bar{x}$ and considering the linearised system $\dot{x} = Ax$ where the so called Jacobian matrix A is defined by $A = f'(\bar{x})$. The linear theory discussed in the previous section is appropriate for this task. An important result for the analysis of nonlinear systems states that in a neighbourhood of the equilibrium point the nonlinear system is topologically equivalent to its linearized form ,see figure 2.10, provided that the Jacobian matrix A does not have pure complex eigenvalues. Thus the various equilibrium points can be classified as stable, unstable or saddle point. Those equilibrium points at which the Jacobian matrix has eigenvalues with nonzero real part are known as *hyperbolic fixed points*. Two phase portraits are topologically equivalent if there is a homoeomorphism (i.e. a mapping which is continuous and one-to-one in both directions) of the state space which maps one of the portraits to the other. Under this homeomorphism integral curves are preserved i.e. spirals are mapped into spirals, closed orbits into closed orbits, saddle-points into saddle points, etc., and the direction of motion along integral curves is also preserved. For a proper mathematical definition we refer the reader to Arnold (1973).

The case when the Jacobian matrix at an equilibrium point has pure complex eigenvalues is precisely the one which introduces a solution concept which does not occur in linear systems. It was Raleigh (1877) who first noticed that certain nonlinear systems could exhibit around an equilibrium point the type of motion exhibited in figure 2.11. For instance in the first diagram the equilibrium point is locally unstable with trajectories which start close to it spiralling towards a closed periodic solution whilst trajectories starting outside this closed periodic solution are spiralling in towards it. The closed periodic solution which is attracting all nearby trajectories is known as a *limit cycle* and may be either stable (as for the case discussed) or unstable (as for the case in the second diagram).

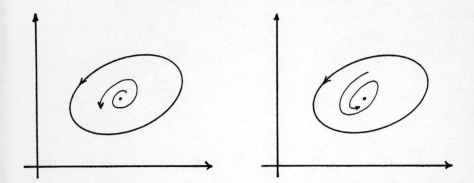

Figure 2.11   Limit cycle motion

The existence of limit cycle motion can be deduced from a study of the linearised system by use of the *Hopf bifurcation theorem*. Suppose the nonlinear system of interest depends on a parameter μ so that we are considering the system

$$\dot{x} = f(x, \mu). \tag{2.6}$$

Let $A(\mu)$ denote the Jacobian matrix around the equilibrium point $\bar{x}$ and suppose that at $\mu = 0$ the eigenvalues of A are pure complex. If the real part of the eigenvalue, $\alpha(\mu)$, depends on μ in such a way that $\alpha'(0) \neq 0$ then a limit cycle exists in a neighbourhood of $\bar{x}$ either for $\mu < 0$ or $\mu > 0$, but not both. The question of the stability of the limit cycle cannot be answered from a study of the linearized system but a number of techniques are available, one of which we shall discuss in a later section.

The Hopf bifurcation theorem provides the classic example of *bifurcation behaviour*. As the parameter μ varies through zero the behaviour of the dynamical system undergoes a qualitative change e.g. from local stability to local instability with motion out to a stable limit cycle. In such instances the value $\mu = 0$ is known as a bifurcation point. An understanding of these is essential for a complete analysis of nonlinear dynamical systems.

What we have said so far does not preclude the possibility that a nonlinear system may display a family of closed orbits around an equilibrium point as is the case for linear systems with pure complex eigenvalues. This would occur when $A(\mu)$ has pure complex eigenvalues for an interval of μ values as is the case for conservative systems of the type $\dot{x} = f(x)$ which are of interest in mechanics.

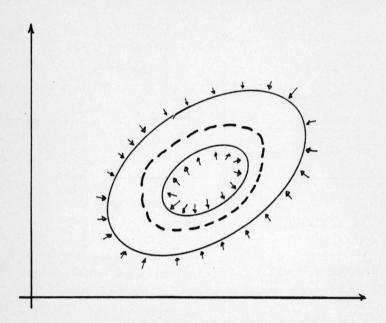

<u>Figure 2.12</u> Poincaré-Bendixson theorem

Once the hyperbolic fixed points of a nonlinear dynamical system have been located and their stability studied the next step is to determine whether the system possesses any limit cycles. The main theorems for this purpose are the Poincaré-Bendixson theorem and Bendixson's Criterion. The *Poincaré-Bendixson theorem* states that if there is a closed annular region of the plane containing no equilibrium points and which has all trajectories entering from one bounding curve or the other then that region contains at least one limit cycle. See figure 2.12. The *Bendixson Criterion* is a simple test which allows us to rule out the possibility of a limit cycle in a simply connected region D of the plane. It states that if the trace of the Jacobian matrix (evaluated at a general point of the region, not merely at an equilibrium point) is nonzero and does not change sign throughout D then there are no closed orbits in D.

A further useful theorem which complements the Bendixson criterion is the *Hartman-Olech theorem* (1963). This theorem states that if at every point in a compact region around an equilibrium point the Jacobian matrix of the system has negative trace and positive determinant then the equilibrium point is globally asymptotically stable.

Having located all the fixed points and closed orbits of the two-dimensional nonlinear system we can appeal to results given by Andronov et al. (1966) which state that the equilibrium sets of the system i.e. those sets in the x-plane which attract all trajectories as time tends to +∞ or -∞ fall into three classes:-

(i)   fixed points,
(ii) closed orbits,
(iii) the unions of fixed points and the trajectories connecting them.

The first two categories are already familiar from what has been discussed earlier. The third category usually include saddle to saddle connections and are referred to as *heteroclinic orbits* when connecting distinct fixed points and *homoclinic orbits* when connecting the same fixed point to itself.   Some of these solution concepts are illustrated in figure 2.13.

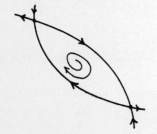

(a)   heteroclinic orbit   (b)   homoclinic orbit

(c)   band of closed orbits

Figure 2.13

A crucial result which distinguishes two-dimensional systems from higher dimensional ones is *Peixoto's theorem* (1962). This theorem which applies to dynamical systems on any compact two-dimensional manifold (and not just to planar systems) states that structurally stable systems must belong to categories (i) and (ii) above. The solution concepts which arise under category (iii) are not really of interest in modelling situations in two dimensions because they are structurally unstable.

During the 1960's mathematicians attempted to find an analogue of Peixoto's theorem for higher dimensional differential systems. This search led to the development of Morse-Smale systems which place certain constraints on the topology of the manifold on which the differential system is evolving; see e.g. Smale (1967) and Markus (1971). The search for a higher dimensional analogue of Peixoto's theorem turned out to be a vain one - the most that it is possible to say is that the special Morse-Smale systems are structurally stable, however it is possible to have structurally stable systems which are not Morse-Smale and furthermore structurally stable systems are not necessarily dense on the manifold of the differential system. The reasons for the lack of a higher dimensional Peixoto's theorem involve some subtle arguments in differential topology and are discussed by Chillingworth (1976) but the essential reason is that there can exist complicated non-wandering sets which cannot be removed by small perturbations. A point p is nonwandering if every neighbourhood U of p, when moving under the influence of the differential system, never ceases to overlap itself, no matter how long the system is allowed to run. The set of nonwandering points forms the nonwandering set.

The importance of the observations in the preceding paragraph for model building using differential systems is that the set of solution concepts arising in two-dimensional nonlinear systems are only a subset of the types of dynamical behaviour that dynamical systems may exhibit. As we shall see in a later section to these we need to add the concept of chaotic motion.

Before proceeding to discuss these additional solution concepts we shall complete our discussion of planar nonlinear systems by discussing some techniques which allow us to say something about the nature of limit cycle solutions.

2.5 Analysis of Limit Cycles

In the previous section we cited the Poincaré-Bendixson theorem which allows us to establish the existence of limit cycles. However for an economic theorist this knowledge is only a first step in the analysis of a dynamic model. Often the object of the analysis is to determine how the parameters of the model or the exogenous variables affect the amplitude and period of the limit cycle. Since even for the simplest text-book examples of limit cycle motion it is impossible to obtain closed form expressions for the equation of the limit cycle, it is clear that some type of approximate method is required. In this section we shall outline the commonest method of approximating limit cycles, namely the *method of averaging*. This method was originally developed by the Soviet mathematicians Krylov and Bogoliubov (1937) in order to obtain precise quantitative estimates of limit cycles. However the development of modern computers has obviated the need for precise quantitative approximation and the method is now used as a means of obtaining qualitative information about limit cycles.

The method of averaging is generally applied to planar nonlinear differential systems in the form

$$\dot{x} = Ax + \epsilon f(x),\tag{2.7}$$

where A is the Jacobian matrix of the nonlinear system evaluated at the equilibrium point $\bar{x}$ around which the limit cycle is known or assumed to exist. Here ϵ is assumed to be a "small" parameter, however we shall have more to say about the small parameter assumption at a later point.

Since the limit cycle involves rotational motion the first step in the application of the method of averaging is to transform equation (2.7) to polar coordinates via the change of variables

$$x_1 = r \cos \theta, \quad x_2 = r \sin \theta.\tag{2.8}$$

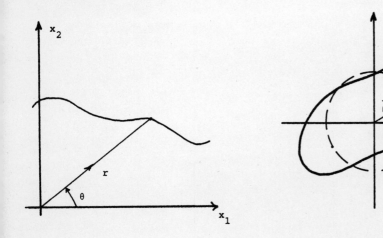

Figure 2.14   Figure 2.15

In terms of these coordinates, illustrated in figure 2.14, the differential system (2.7) becomes

$$\dot{r} = r(a_{11}\cos^2\theta + a_{22}\sin^2\theta + (a_{12} + a_{21})\cos\theta\sin\theta)$$
$$\text{(2.9)}$$
$$+ \epsilon(g_1(r,\theta)\cos\theta + g_2(r,\theta)\sin\theta), \tag{2.9}$$

and

$$\dot{\theta} = a_{21}\cos^2\theta - a_{12}\sin^2\theta + (a_{22} - a_{11})\sin\theta\cos\theta$$
$$\text{(2.10)}$$
$$+ \epsilon(g_2(r,\theta)\cos\theta - g_1(r,\theta)\sin\theta)/r.$$

For convenience we have introduced the notation

$$g_i(r,\theta) = f_i(r\cos\theta, r\sin\theta)$$

for i=1,2.

The right-hand sides of equations (2.9) and (2.10) are periodic in θ and may be approximated to any desired degree of accuracy by a Fourier expansion. The first term of this expansion is obtained by averaging the right-hand sides of the differential equations with respect to θ on the interval $[0,2\pi]$. In this way we obtain the averaged equations

$$\dot{\rho} = \rho\,\text{tr}(A)/2 + \epsilon G(\rho), \tag{2.11}$$

and

$$\dot{\varphi} = (a_{21} - a_{12})/2 + \epsilon H(\rho)/\rho, \tag{2.12}$$

where

$$G(\rho) = \frac{1}{2\pi}\int_0^{2\pi}(g_1(\rho,\theta)\cos\theta + g_2(\rho,\theta)\sin\theta)\,d\theta, \tag{2.13}$$

and

$$H(\rho) = \frac{1}{2\pi}\int_0^{2\pi}(g_2(\rho,\theta)\cos\theta - g_1(\rho,\theta)\sin\theta)\,d\theta. \tag{2.14}$$

The quantities ρ and φ are the first order approximations to r and θ respectively. The equilibrium point of equation (2.11), $\bar{\rho}$ say, is a circle in the x-plane which approximates the limit cycle as shown in figure 2.15.

The accuracy of the approximation is improved by taking higher order terms in the Fourier expansion of the right-hand sides of equations (2.9) and (2.10). However for a qualitative analysis of the amplitude of the limit cycle the averaged equation (2.11) is adequate.

Most standard discussions of the method of averaging, as for example that of Guckenheimer and Holmes (1983), make use of the fact that ϵ is a small parameter and seek an expansion in terms of powers of ϵ. Since in many of our applications there is no obvious "small" parameter we have prefered instead to use the Fourier expansion concept which is in keeping with Aiserman's method of equivalent linearization. This latter method was in fact devised to avoid the need for small parameter arguments and is more fully discussed by Minorsky (1962). It is also conventional to use the transformation z = Px discussed in section 2.3 to transform equation (2.7) into a form where the matrix A has the canonical form of equation (2.3). This approach has the advantage that the first term in the differential equation for ϕ is β (=(det(A) - tr(A)^2/4)$^{1/2}$) which is the period of the linearized motion. The disadvantage of this approach is that G becomes a far more complicated function of the parameters of the model so that qualitative analysis of the limit cycle is rendered far more difficult. If we were seeking accurate quantitative information then the issue of which approximation is closer to the actual solution would be relevant. However the object of our analysis is qualitative information about the determinants of the limit cycle and so this issue is not important. In chapter 5 we shall illustrate the standard approach on a simple extension to Goodwin's model, where it turns out that the function G is uncharacteristically of a simple form.

As a simple example of the mechanics of applying the method of averaging we consider the differential system

$$\tau\dot{x} = -x -y -k\varphi(x), \tag{2.15}$$

$$\dot{y} = x, \tag{2.16}$$

where the function $\varphi(x)$ has the symmetrical shape shown in figure 2.16. The assumptions on φ are that $\varphi(0) = 0$, $\varphi' < 0$, $\varphi''(0) = 0$, sign $\varphi''(x) =$ sign x and $\varphi'(x) \to 0$ as $x \to \pm\infty$.

In equation (2.15) the parameter τ which multiplies the $\dot{x}$ plays the role of a time lag which shall be allowed to tend to zero in our discussion on relaxation oscillations in the next section.

Our choice of the system (2.15-16) is not arbitrary, it can be reduced to Lienard's (1928) equation which is the exemplar of limit cycle motion on the plane. Many of the nonlinear models we consider in later chapters can be reduced to a version of this system.

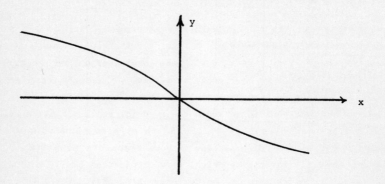

Figure 2.16   The function y = ϕ(x)

In the x-y plane the equilibrium point of the differential system (2.15-16) is determined by the intersection of the y-axis and the curve y - f(x) - -x -kφ(x). This curve is monotonic decreasing for k < -1/φ'(0) and has two turning points for k > -1/φ'(0), both cases being illustrated in figure 2.17.

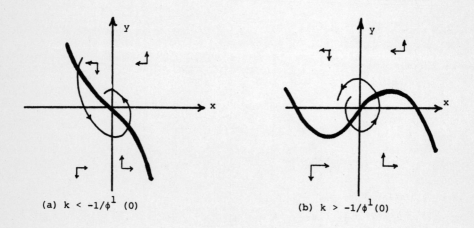

(a) k < -1/ϕ^1(0)   (b) k > -1/ϕ^1(0)

Figure 2.17

If we define the parameter ϵ - -(1 + kφ'(0))/τ, the function g by

$$g(x) = \varphi'(0)x - \varphi(x),\qquad\qquad(2.17)$$

and the matrix A by

$$A = \begin{bmatrix} \epsilon & -1/\tau \\ 1 & 0 \end{bmatrix},\qquad\qquad(2.18)$$

then the differential system (2.15-16) may be written

$$\begin{bmatrix} \dot{x} \\ \dot{y} \end{bmatrix} \quad A \begin{bmatrix} x \\ y \end{bmatrix} + \frac{k}{\tau} \begin{bmatrix} g(x) \\ 0 \end{bmatrix}.\qquad\qquad(2.19)$$

We note that $\det(A) = 1/\tau > 0$ and $\text{tr}(A) = \epsilon$. Hence if we consider the qualitative behaviour of the differential system (2.19) as the parameter k increases past $-1/\varphi'(0)$ (i.e. as ϵ increases through 0) we see that the equlibrium point at the origin switches from being locally stable (for $\epsilon < 0$) to being locally unstable (for $\epsilon > 0$). Furthermore we know from our earlier discussion of the Hopf bifurcation theorem that a limit cycle exists on one side of $\epsilon = 0$. The method of averaging will give us information about the stability and determinants of the limit cycle.

Straightforward application of equation (2.11) yields for the approximate radius vector the differential equation

$$\dot{\rho} = (k\ h(\rho) - \rho)/2\tau,\qquad\qquad(2.20)$$

where the function h is defined by

$$h(\rho) = -\frac{1}{\pi}\int_0^{2\pi} \varphi(\rho\cos\theta)\cos\theta\ d\theta.\qquad\qquad(2.21)$$

In appendix 2.1 we show that the function h has the following properties (i) $h'(\rho) > 0$, (ii) $h''(\rho) < 0$, (iii) $h(0) = 0$, (iv) $h'(0) = -\varphi'(0)$ and (v) $h'(\infty) = 0$. The graph of h is displayed in figure 2.18 and it is clear that we need to consider two cases :- (a) the case of local stability, $\epsilon < 0$, when the functions ρ/k and $h(\rho)$ intersect only at $\rho = 0$; in this case $\dot{\rho} < 0$ for all ρ and so the equlibrium is globally as well as locally asymptotically stable, and, (b) the case of local instability, $\epsilon > 0$, when the functions ρ/k and $h(\rho)$ intersect at the points $\rho = 0$ and $\rho = \bar{\rho}$ given by

$$h(\rho) = \rho/k.\qquad\qquad(2.22)$$

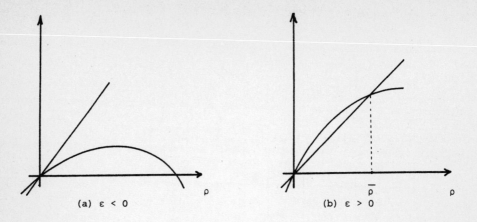

(a) $\varepsilon < 0$ (b) $\varepsilon > 0$

Figure 2.18 The function h

Since $\dot{\rho} < 0$ (>0) for $\rho > \bar{\rho}$ (< $\bar{\rho}$) the limit cycle at $\bar{\rho}$ is asymptotically stable.

For the purposes of our discussion in the next section it is useful to view the x-y phase trajectories on the same diagram as the function $y = f(x)$. This is done in figure 2.17, together with the usual techniques of using arrows to indicate the directions of the vectorfield.

It is worth reflecting on the role played by the assumptions on the function φ in obtaining the above results. The assumption $\varphi'(\infty) = 0$ ensures that $h'(\infty) = 0$ which guarantees at least one nontrivial point of intersection between the function h and the line ρ/k, when $\varepsilon > 0$. The assumptions on φ'' ensure that $h'' < 0$ over its entire domain, hence ensuring a unique nontrivial point of intersection. If these assumptions are relaxed then multiple points of intersection could occur. Each of those would correspond to a limit cycle.

2.6 Relaxation Oscillations

In previous sections we have emphasised that limit cycle solutions become possible once we consider nonlinearities in the differential equations governing the model under consideration. As well as the nonlinearity another important factor influencing the behaviour of many dynamic economic models are time lags (or speed of adjustment parameters which are the inverse of time lags). In many models of interest it is important to understand what happens to the dynamic behaviour as a time lag tends to zero (or a speed of adjustment tends to infinity) and indeed this point turns out to be very important in our discussion of the dynamic instability problem in chapter seven below.

In many such models the time lag occurs on one of the derivative terms of the differential system so that when the time lag is put to zero the dimension of the system is decreased by one. If careful attention is not paid to the "lost" dimension perverse conclusions about stability may be drawn when viewing the model exclusively in the lower dimension. As an example of such a system consider again the set of differential equations (2.15-16) and interpret the parameter τ as a time lag. If the time lag is assumed to be zero then x and y are constrained to lie on the curve

$$y = f(x) = - x - k\, \varphi(x), \tag{2.23}$$

with dynamic motion governed by

$$f(\dot{y}) = y. \tag{2.24}$$

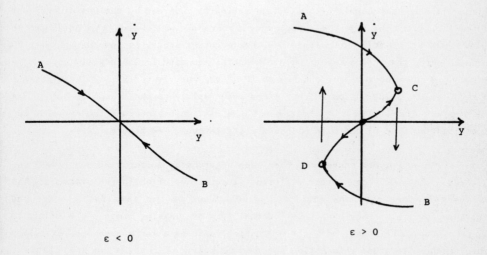

Figure 2.19 Looking at the motion on a one-dimensional manifold

The graph of this relationship, which we write $\dot{y} = F(y)$, is shown in figure 2.19 for both the cases $\epsilon < 0$ and $\epsilon > 0$. The dynamics in the case $\epsilon < 0$ are clear enough, since $\dot{y} > 0$ (< 0) for $y < 0$ (> 0), motion is along the curve AB towards the equilibrium point at the origin O. The dynamics in the case $\epsilon > 0$ present more of a problem, all motion flows to the points C or D but motion cannot be stationary there since these are not equilibrium points of the differential equation (2.24). It may seem tempting to impose some kind of jump hypothesis on the motion to allow phase points to jump from C onto the lower branch BD or from D to the upper branch AC. It turns out that this is indeed the behaviour but further analysis is needed to explain how a differential equation whose motion is restricted to the one-dimensional manifold $\dot{y} = F(y)$ can become two-dimensional.

A proper understanding of the dynamics is obtained by expressing equation (2.15) in the form.

$$\dot{x} = (f(x) - y)/\tau. \tag{2.25}$$

We first observe that $\dot{x} < 0$ (>0) at points in the phase plane where $y > f(x)$ ($< f(x)$). As $\tau \downarrow 0$ the derivative $\dot{x}$ tends to infinity except in a neighbourhood of the curve $y = f(x)$ where motion is governed by the one dimensional differential equation (2.24). Now consider how the motion evolves from the arbitrary initial point I in figure 2.20. The variable x moves very rapidly and almost horizontally (indeed instantaneously and horizontally in the limit $\tau = 0$) to a neighbourhood of the curve $y = f(x)$ where motion is governed by the one-dimensional equation (2.24). In the case $\epsilon < 0$ trajectories are swept towards the equilibrium point at the origin. In the case $\epsilon > 0$ trajectories are swept towards the point D from which under the influence of the differential equation (2.25) x again moves very rapidly to a neighbourhood of the branch AC of the curve $y = f(x)$, trajectories are then swept to the point C from which x jumps very rapidly to the branch BD and so the cycle repeats itself. In the limit $\tau = 0$ the limit cycle becomes the curve CC'DD' with motion from C to C' and D to D' being instantaneous; see figure 2.21.

The geometric arguments above have been made rigorous by Andronov et al. (1966) who proved for a class of second order differential equations of which the system (2.15) is a special case, that the qualitative behaviour is the same for τ small and positive as for $\tau = 0$. They have labelled this type of limiting limit cycle motion a discontinuous oscillation and their discussion contains a large number of examples. In more recent literature this motion has become known as relaxation oscillation, which is a less descriptive but now dominant terminology.

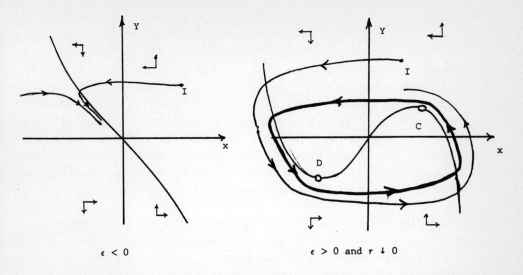

Figure 2.20 Looking at the motion on a two-dimensional manifold

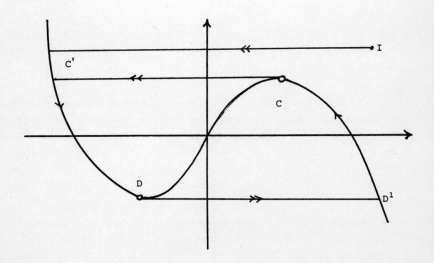

Figure 2.21 The limiting limit cycle - discontinuous oscillation

2.7 **Higher Dimensional Nonlinear Systems**

Now consider the n-dimensional nonlinear differential equation $\dot{x} = f(x)$. We know from Hartman's theorem, discussed in section 2.2, that the linearization of this equation around an equilibrium point determines the qualitative behaviour locally provided the Jacobian matrix A has no eigenvalues with zero real part. Thus any essentially local nonlinear behaviour such as limit cycles will be connected with the eigenvalues of A having zero real part. The basic tool used to analyse such systems is the *centre manifold theorem* which is a generalization of the idea of decoupling linear systems via the Jordan canonical form discussed in section 2.3.

The centre manifold theorem is stated in full detail by Guckenheimer and Holmes (1983). However we shall describe the theory for the special case when A only has eigenvalues with negative and zero real part. In terms of notation introduced earlier we may say that the motion of the linear part of the differential equation is spanned by a stable and a centre manifold of dimension k and l respectively where k + l = n. By appropriate transformations the given differential equation can be written in the form

$$\dot{z} = S\,z + F(z,y),$$

$$\dot{y} = C\,y + G(z,y),$$

(2.26)

where $z \in \mathbf{R}^k$, $y \in \mathbf{R}^l$ and S and C are k x k and l x l matrices whose eigenvalues have negative real parts and zero real parts respectively. The centre manifold theorem asserts that the flow of the differential system (2.26) is attracted to the centre manifold

$$z = h(y),$$

(2.27)

and that motion on this manifold is determined by the differential equation

$$\dot{y} = C\,y + G(h(y),y).$$

(2.28)

Furthermore the centre manifold goes through the equilibrium point and is tangential to the centre manifold of the linearised system there. These ideas are illustrated in figures 2.22-23. The difficult task in centre manifold theory is to obtain an expression for h. To do so exactly would amount to knowing the solution of the original differential equation. However a number of techniques for finding reasonable approximations to h based on Taylor expansions exist and we shall illustrate these

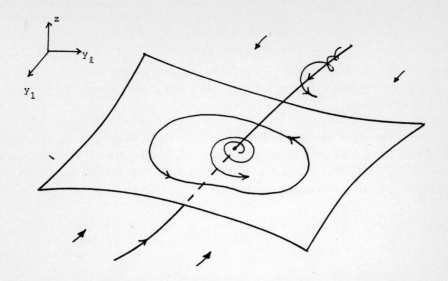

Figure 2.22 Motion around and on the centre manifold

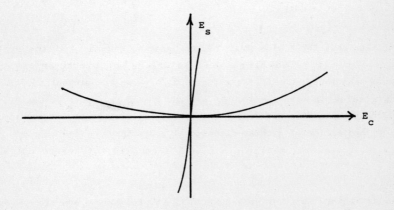

Figure 2.23 Relation of centre manifold to linear eigenspaces

when we apply the centre manifold theorem to a version of Goodwin's (1967) fluctuating growth model in chapter five.

Typically centre manifold analysis uncovers limit cycle motion in higher dimensional systems. Have we now exhausted the types of behaviour which a nonlinear system is capable of exhibiting ?

The failure of Peixoto's theorem to generalize beyond two dimensions gives the clue that far more complicated motion is possible in higher dimensional differential systems. In the early 1960's Lorenz (1963) obtained computer solutions of the three dimensional nonlinear differential system

$$\dot{x} = -\sigma x + \sigma y,$$
$$\dot{y} = rx - y \qquad - xz, \qquad\qquad (2.29)$$
$$\dot{z} = \qquad - bz + xy,$$

where σ, r and b are positive constants. Lorenz was led to study this differential system as part of a research program into the unpredictable nature of weather patterns.

Lorenz noticed that for a wide range of the parameters (σ, r, b) the system (2.29) which is only mildly nonlinear has solutions exhibiting an extraordinarily complicated behaviour. For instance figure 2.24 shows the projection onto the (x, z) plane of a solution when $\sigma = 10$, $b = 8/3$ and $r = 28$. It must be borne in mind that the trajectory shown does not really intersect itself since we are looking at a two-dimensional projection of a three-dimensional trajectory.

The characteristics that give the motion its complicated, or so called chaotic, behaviour, are:

(i)   The trajectory is recurrent, continuing to wind around and around, jumping from one loop to the other, but without ever settling down to either periodic or stationary behaviour. (A dynamical system is said to be recurrent if for any neighbourhood U of the state space, each trajectory recurs or passes through that neighbourhood again and again as $t \to + \infty$ or $- \infty$. A good example is solenoidal flow on a torus.)

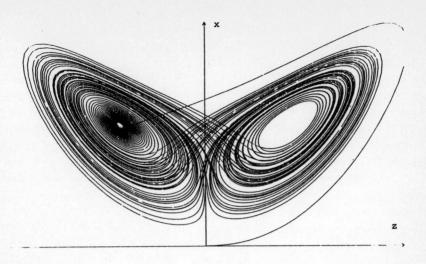

Figure 2.24   The Lorenz attractor

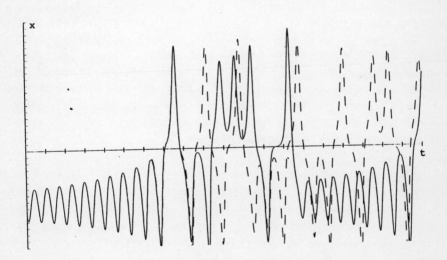

Figure 2.25   Paths of the Lorenz equation from nearby initial values

(ii) The general form of the figure does not depend on the initial conditions, apart from an initial transient section.

(iii) The exact details of the motion depend critically upon the initial values. The sequence in which the two loops are traversed changes dramatically for small changes in initial values. As a consequence it is not possible to predict how a particular trajectory will evolve over anything other than a very short time interval. The meaning we attach to unpredictability in this context is that any small error in the measurement of the current initial position eventually leads to total ignorance of the position of the state variable within the chaotic attractor.

In figure 2.25 we plot two trajectories having initial values differing by 10^{-2} units over the time interval t = 0 to 100. The difference in the two solutions is quite marked.

A consequence of property (iii) is that any imprecision in initial values makes long term prediction of any particular trajectory impossible, even though we can have a qualitative view of the motion as a whole. We shall see that this point is quite important when we come to discuss the dynamics of perfect foresight models in chapter 7.

Differential systems such as (2.29) are called chaotic systems and the complicated limit set to which trajectories are converging, such as figure 2.24 are known as strange attractors. The interest of such systems derives from the fact that though they are deterministic the behaviour of particular solutions is unpredictable, in other words stochastic. An understanding of chaotic behaviour becomes particularly important in light of the assertion (yet to be proved) by Orsay & McLaughlin (1980) that chaotic behaviour is generic for nonlinear dynamical systems i.e. most nonlinear systems can be expected to display chaotic behaviour.

A full discussion of the Lorenz equations is given by Sparrow (1982) and some other prototype three-dimensional chaotic differential systems are presented in Rössler (1979). In all of these systems chaotic behaviour usually arises in one of two ways. The first is due to the existence of heteroclinic or homoclinic orbits. It will be recalled that it is the fact that such orbits persist under arbitrary perturbations which prevents the generalization of Peixoto's theorem to manifolds of dimension greater than two. The second route to chaos, and this is the one we shall encounter, is period doubling. Typically a limit cycle is born as a parameter passes through a bifurcation value and as the parameter increases the period of the limit cycle continues to double, until beyond a critical value the period becomes infinite. From this point the system is displaying chaotic behaviour, the motion is bounded, recurrent but *not* periodic (infinite period means it takes an infinite time for the motion to repeat itself). The period doubling to chaos sequence is illustrated in figure 2.26.

Many of the known examples of period doubling to chaos occur in one-dimensional nonlinear difference equations and in chapter six we show how this behaviour can occur in the cobweb model. A thorough discussion of chaotic motion in models of economic dynamics is given by Lorenz (1989).

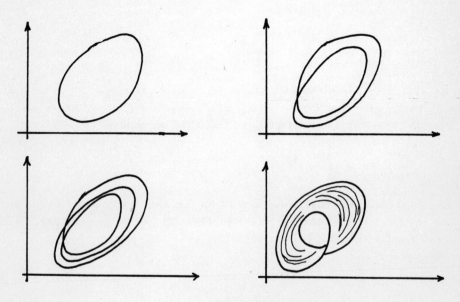

Figure 2.26

Appendix 2.1

From equation (2.21)

$$h(0) = -\frac{1}{\pi} \int_0^{2\pi} \varphi(0) \cos \theta \, d\theta = 0$$

since $\varphi(0) = 0$.

Differentiating equation (2.21) we find

$$h'(\rho) = -\frac{1}{\pi} \int_0^{2\pi} \varphi'(\rho \cos \theta) \cos^2\theta \, d\theta > 0,$$

given that the function $\varphi' < 0$ over its entire domain. Setting $\rho = 0$ in the last equation we readily find that $h'(0) = -\varphi'(0)$. The property $\varphi'(\pm\infty) = 0$ leads easily to the result $h'(\infty) = 0$. Differentiating the last equation we have

$$h''(\rho) = -\frac{1}{\pi} \int_0^{2\pi} \varphi''(\rho \cos \theta) \cos^3\theta \, d\theta.$$

Recalling the assumptions that $\varphi''(x) < 0$ (> 0) for $x < 0$ (> 0) and $\varphi''(0) = 0$ and considering the integral over the subintervals $(0, \pi/2)$, $(\pi/2, \pi)$, $(\pi, 3\pi/2)$ and $(3\pi/2, 2\pi)$ we readily find that $h''(\rho) < 0$.

CHAPTER 3 **A NEW LOOK AT SOME OLD ENDOGENEOUS CYCLE THEORIES**

3.1 **Introduction**

In chapter one we mentioned that there are two broad approaches to business cycle theory - the endogenous cycle theories and the exogenous shock theories. In this chapter we shall use the concepts and techniques of the previous chapter to place a class of endogenous cycle theories into a unified mathematical framework. In particular we shall be considering theories whose basis is in the dynamics of the real sector. This emphasis in no way indicates a belief that these theories are the unique or most satisfactory explanation of the business cycle. Our choice is dictated partly by the fact that these theories provide a well recognized body of economic knowledge which can benefit from a unified viewpoint and partly by the fact that they are still seen as the most representative of the endogenous cycle theories.

There have been a number of elegant mathematical treatments of some of the traditional cycle theories e.g. the treatment of Kaldor's model by Chang and Smyth (1971) and Schinasi (1982) and of a complete Keynesian system by Torre (1977). These treatments concentrated on the question of the existence of limit cycles and consequently made use of Poincaré-Bendixson theory. Our aim is to go beyond the existence question and to characterise the properties of the cycle, in particular to determine how the amplitude of the cycle is affected by model parameters and policy variables. To this end our main tool will be the method of averaging which was expounded in the last chapter. It should be pointed out that the use of the method of averaging in economic analysis was suggested by Bothwell (1952) in the early post-war years. However the use of the method did not become widespread from that time partly because Bothwell's treatment was rooted in the frequency-response techniques of electrical engineering which are not well suited to the type of qualitative analysis required for economic theory - also partly because the interest of economic theorists was starting to swing towards the exogenous shock theories. Now, some thirty years later, there is still no clear verdict between the endogenous cycle theories and exogenous shock theories as evidenced by the recent studies of Blatt (1983), Mullineux (1984) and Zarnowitz (1985). Indeed Blatt presents strong arguments against the exogenous shock theories and Zarnowitz states "There is not much empirical validation that random shocks of all kinds play as large a role in business cycles as has been attributed to them in recent literature. The weight of exogenous policy factors, too, seems more often than not overstated." So the time seems ripe for a unified framework in which to discuss endogenous cycle theories so that the substantive use of nonlinearities in business cycle theory, called for by Zarnowitz, can be explored. The rekindling of interest in endogenous cycle theories occurs at a time when developments in the qualitative theory of dynamical systems sketched in the previous chapter place in the hands of economic theorists a set of tools and concepts far better suited to the task of developing business cycle models than was the case when Bothwell made his contribution.

A good modern discussion of business cycle theories is given by Gabisch and Lorenz (1989) whilst a discussion of endogenous cycle theories along the lines presented here is given by Medio (1979).

3.2   A General Model of Multiplier-Accelerator Interactions

We consider a goods market model where aggregate demand for output is given by

$$Z = C + I + G, \tag{3.1}$$

here C, I and G represent consumption, investment and government spending. We assume that supply of output adjusts with a lag to excess demand, so that

$$\dot{Y} = \frac{1}{T_o} (Z - Y) , \tag{3.2}$$

where T_o is the output lag and Y represents output. Substituting (3.1) into (3.2) and making the standard assumption $C = cY$ $(0 < c < 1)$, we can express (3.2) in the form

$$T_o \dot{Y} + sY - G = I , \tag{3.3}$$

where $s = 1 - c$.

The dynamics of such aggregate demand models are heavily influenced by the form of the investment function. A fairly general investment function which would encompass a large number discussed in the literature on multiplier-accelerator type models is of the form

$$I(t) = \int_{-\infty}^{t} e^{-\gamma(t-s)} B(Y(s), \dot{Y}(s)) \, ds \qquad (3.4)$$

where $B(Y(t), \dot{Y}(t))$ is the new investment at time t and γ is a positive constant. Equation (3.4) shows total investmment at time t as a declining weighted average of all past investment decisions, reflecting the fact that the effect of some investment decisions is felt only after a certain time delay. Setting $T_i = 1/\gamma$ equation (4) may also be written in the form

$$T_i \dot{I} + I = B(Y, \dot{Y}). \qquad (3.5)$$

Here T_i may be interpreted as the average investment lag. Substituting into equation (3.5) the expression for I given by equation (3.3) we find that Y satisfies the second order nonlinear differential equation

$$T_i T_o \ddot{Y} + (sT_i + T_o) \dot{Y} + sY - B(Y, \dot{Y}) = T_i \dot{G} + G. \qquad (3.6)$$

In this preliminary analysis we shall assume that government spending G is held constant and hence ignore the effect of a changing government spending policy G, save to say that its effect on the differential equation is as a forcing term on the right hand side. This effect may not be as simple to predict as the once and for all type changes in G familiar from comparative static analysis. We shall return to analyse the effect of this forcing term later in the chapter.

We are thus reduced to analysing the differential equation

$$T_i T_o \ddot{Y} + (sT_i + T_o) \dot{Y} + sY - B(Y, \dot{Y}) = G, \qquad (3.7)$$

whose equilibrium point $\bar{Y}$ is given by

$$s\bar{Y} - B(\bar{Y}, 0) = G. \qquad (3.8)$$

Defining $y = Y - \bar{Y}$, $\mu = 1/T_i T_0$, subtracting (3.8) from (3.7) and performing some rearrangements we are led to analyse the nonlinear differential equation

$$\ddot{y} + \mu(sT_i + T_0)\dot{y} + s\mu y - \mu b(y, \dot{y}) = 0, \qquad (3.9)$$

where

$$b(y, \dot{y}) = B(y + \bar{Y}, \dot{y}) - B(\bar{Y}, 0). \qquad (3.10)$$

Explicitly removing the linear parts from the nonlinear $b(y, \dot{y})$ term we may express (3.9) in the form

$$\ddot{y} + \mu(sT_i + T_0 - b_2)\dot{y} + \mu(s - b_1)y - \mu\, e(y, \dot{y}) = 0 \qquad (3.11)$$

where we define $b_1 = B_1(\bar{Y}, 0)$, $b_2 = B_2(\bar{Y}, 0)$ (subscripts indicating partial derivatives) and

$$e(y, \dot{y}) = b(y, \dot{y}) - b_1 y - b_2 \dot{y}. \qquad (3.12)$$

The standard linearised model is analysed by setting the term $e(y, \dot{y}) = 0$. The linearised differential equation has characteristic equation

$$\lambda^2 + \mu(sT_i + T_0 - b_2)\lambda + \mu(s - b_1) = 0. \qquad (3.13)$$

Letting λ_1, λ_2 represent the roots of this equation we note first of all that $\lambda_1\lambda_2 = s - b_1$ which is > 0, thereby ruling out saddle point behaviour at the equilibrium $(\bar{Y}, 0)$, if $s > b_1$. We shall only consider this case, which corresponds to the standard Keynesian assumption that the savings function is steeper than the investment function. The case $\lambda_1\lambda_2 < 0$ is not devoid of interest but requires a different type of analysis which would take us beyond the scope of the present book. The local stability of the equilibrium point then hinges on the sum of the roots

$$\lambda_1 + \lambda_2 = \mu(b_2 - sT_i - T_0), \qquad (3.14)$$

with the equilibrium being locally stable for $b_2 < sT_i + T_0$ and locally unstable for $b_2 > sT_i + T_0$. Defining $\varepsilon = b_2 - sT_i - T_0$ it is clear that $\varepsilon = 0$ is a bifurcation point and application of the Hopf-bifurcation theorem indicates the existence of limit cycle motion as ε passes through zero (this follows since (dλ/dε) evaluated at ε = 0 equals −μ/2 ≠ 0).

In order to analyse the limit cycle we first express the second order differential equation in matrix form by setting $x_1 = y$ and $x_2 = \dot{y}$, which satisfy

$$
\begin{bmatrix} \dot{x}_1 \\ \dot{x}_2 \end{bmatrix} = \begin{bmatrix} 0 & 1 \\ -\mu(s-b_1) & \mu\varepsilon \end{bmatrix} \begin{bmatrix} x_1 \\ x_2 \end{bmatrix} + \mu \begin{bmatrix} 0 \\ e(x_1, x_2) \end{bmatrix} . \tag{3.15}
$$

Applying the method of averaging as outlined in the last chapter we find that the radius vector of the first order approximation to the limit cycle satisfies the differential equation

$$
\dot{\rho} = \frac{\mu}{2}(\varepsilon\rho + V(\rho)), \tag{3.16}
$$

where

$$
V(\rho) = \frac{1}{\pi} \int_0^{2\pi} e(\rho\cos\theta,\ \rho\sin\theta)\ \sin\theta\ d\theta. \tag{3.17}
$$

Notice that if we ignore the nonlinear element $V(\rho)$ in equation (3.16) then the resulting differential equation is nothing more than the linearised version of the model, transformed to polar coordinates. Nonlinear effects are captured (to first order) by the nonlinear element $V(\rho)$. Various endogenous cycle models of the class we are considering differ in this nonlinear term.

3.3 Goodwin's Nonlinear Accelerator Model

In this model, first analysed by Goodwin (1951), the investment function is assumed to be a nonlinear function of $\dot{Y}$ only, i.e.

$$
B(Y, \dot{Y}) = B(\dot{Y}) , \tag{3.18}
$$

with the general shape shown in Figure 3.1. This particular investment function reflects constraints on investment and disinvestment. Here L is an upper capacity constraint on investment and M is a lower bound on the scrapping rate of capital equipment. Before analysing some particular models it is worth pointing out that

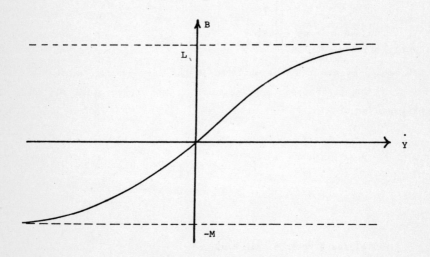

Figure 3.1 Goodwin's nonlinear accelerator

the differential system (3.15) is of the same general form as the prototype example (2.19) considered in the last chapter. Here we have a slightly more general nonlinear term. In the prototype example of chapter 2 we showed how to analyse the limiting discontinuous oscillation when one of the differential equations of the system collapses into an algebraic equation. A similar case arises here when one or other of the time lags T_i or T_0 tends to zero.

The middle section of the investment function has slope close to v, corresponding to the standard linear accelerator $B(\dot{Y}) = v\dot{Y}$.

Note first of all that from equation (3.8),

$$\bar{Y} = G/s. \tag{3.19}$$

From equation (3.12) and (3.17) the expression for $V(\rho)$ reduces to

$$V(\rho) = H(\rho) - v\rho, \tag{3.20}$$

where

$$H(\rho) = \frac{1}{\pi} \int_0^{2\pi} B(\rho \sin \theta) \sin \theta \, d\theta. \tag{3.21}$$

Thus the differential equation (3.16) assumes the form

$$\dot{\rho} = \frac{\mu}{2}(H(\rho) - (sT_i + T_0)\rho). \tag{3.22}$$

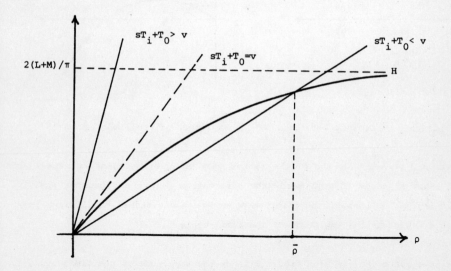

Figure 3.2 The function H and determination of $\bar{\rho}$

We show in appendix 3.1 that for $B(Y)$ having the general shape in figure 3.1, $H(\rho)$ must have the general shape shown in figure 3.2. On the same diagram we sketch the straight line $(sT_i + T_0)\rho$ for $(sT_i + T_0) > v$ and $(sT_i + T_0) < v$. We see from equation (3.22) that the equilibrium points of the differential equation for ρ are given by the intersection of the line $(sT_i + T_0)\rho$ and $H(\rho)$. For $(sT_i + T_0) \geq v$ (i.e. $\varepsilon \leq 0$), the only equilibrium point is $\rho = 0$, but for $(sT_i + T_0) < v$ (i.e. $\varepsilon > 0$)

there are two equilibrium points, $\rho = 0$ and $\rho = \bar{\rho}$, the latter being a first approximation to the amplitude of the limit cycle. An alternative diagram which contains the same information as figure 3.2 but also enables us to determine the stability of the limit cycle is obtained by plotting $\dot{\rho}$ as a functon of ρ from equation (3.22). This graph is obtained by considering that of $H(\rho) - (sT_i + T_0)\rho$ and is shown in figure 3.3 where the cases $\varepsilon \leq 0$ (figure 3.3a) and $\varepsilon > 0$ (figure 3.3b) are displayed.

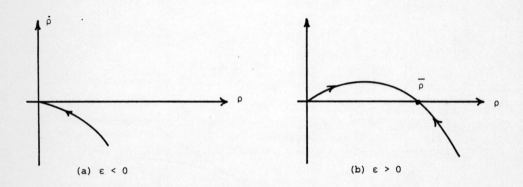

(a) $\varepsilon < 0$ (b) $\varepsilon > 0$

Figure 3.3 Dynamic behaviour of the amplitude of the limit cycle

From figure 3.3 we see that the origin is the only equilibrium point for $\varepsilon < 0$ and is stable. As ε passes through zero (the bifurcation point) and becomes positive the origin becomes an unstable equilibrium point and a new stable equilibrium point emerges at $\bar{\rho}$, which is the amplitude of the limit cycle.

It is a simple matter to see from figure 3.2 how the amplitude of the limit cycle is affected by changes in parameters of the model. Thus, since the function H is independent of the parameters s, T_i and T_0, we see that the amplitude of the cycle is a decreasing function of these parameters.

The effect of a change in v is determined by considering the effect on the function B. Thus if the effect of an increase in v is to increase B in absolute value at every point of its domain then H is increased over every point of its domain and so the amplitude of the limit cycle is increased.

When the time lags are small we are in the situation of relaxation oscillations discussed in section 2.6 and consequently a different analysis is required. In fact the analysis of the relaxation oscillation inherent in Goodwin's model parallels almost exactly that of section 2.6, the only essential difference being the manner in which the parameters of the model affect the function f in figure 2.21.

To find the appropriate form of the function f for Goodwin's model note that the differential system (3.15) assumes the form

$$\dot{x}_1 = x_2, \tag{3.23}$$

$$T_i T_0 \dot{x}_2 = -sx_1 - (sT_i + T_0)x_2 + B(x_2). \tag{3.24}$$

We know from the discussion of section 2.6 that the equation of the function determining the relaxation oscillation, or the limiting limit cycle, in the case T_i or $T_0 \to 0$ is obtained from equation (3.24) and is given by

$$x_1 = \frac{-(sT_i + T_0)}{s} x_2 + \frac{1}{s} B(x_2) = f(x_2). \tag{3.25}$$

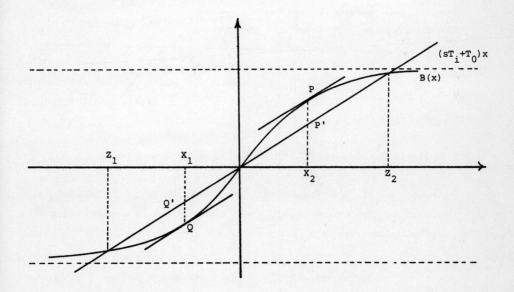

Figure 3.4 Determination of the amplitude of the relaxation oscillation

The properties of the function f are easily obtained by referring to figure 3.4 where the function $B(x)$ and the line $(sT_i + T_0)x$ are sketched. The intersection points of these curves give the intersection points of f with the horizontal axis, namely the origin and the points Z_1 and Z_2. The turning points of f occur at the points X_1, X_2 where B has slope $(sT_i + T_0)$. In the case $T_i \to 0$, the points Z_1, Z_2, X_1 and X_2 are independent of s. Whereas when $T_0 \to 0$ the points Z_1, Z_2, X_1 and X_2 move closer to the origin as s increases. At the same time the maximum and minimum of f (the distances PP' and QQ' respectively in figure 3.4) shrink in absolute value. The function f and the limiting limit cycle are sketched in figure 3.5 for two values of sT_i, the curve labelled ℓ being for a larger value of this parameter. The amplitude of the limiting limit cycle decreasing as sT_i increases. In either case the oscillatory motion of y as a function of time becomes more jerky as the relaxation oscillation limit $(T_i \to 0$ or $T_0 \to 0)$ is approached and this effect is illustrated in figure 3.6.

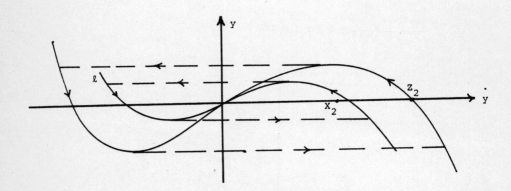

Figure 3.5 The effect of s on the relaxation oscillation

When deriving equation (3.7) we assumed that government spending G is held constant. Now let us determine the effect on the limit cycle of the government pursuing a classical countercyclical spending policy. Such a policy is given by

$$G(t) = \bar{G} - \omega(Y - \bar{Y}) \quad (\omega > 0) \tag{3.26}$$

which indicates that the level of government spending rises (falls) when output Y falls (rises) below the equilibrium level $\bar{Y}$. The positive parameter ω measures the

extent to which the government reacts to fluctuations around the equilibrium level.
Turnovsky (1977) calls this policy a Phillips proportional stabilization policy.

Substituting (3.26) into (3.6) we again arrive at (3.11) but with s now replaced by
s' = s + ω. Hence the effect of the countercyclical government policy is equivalent
to an increase in the savings ratio which as we have seen tends to reduce the
amplitude of the limit cycle. So certainly within this classical Keynesian
framework the countercyclical spending policy is effective in reducing the
fluctuation of the business cycle. It is clearly possible to employ our approach to
analyse the other Phillips stabilization policies discussed by Turnovsky.

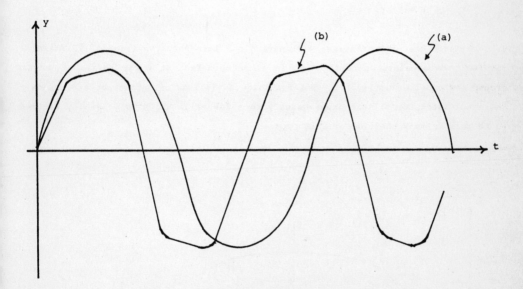

Figure 3.6 (a) Close to the bifurcation point
           (b) Close to the relaxation oscillation limit

In our discussion of the nonlinear accelerator we have followed the formulation of
Allen (1967) who only analyses the cases $T_i = 0$, $T_0 = 0$ and suggests analogue
computer solutions for the general case. Goodwin's own version contained fixed
investment lags instead of the continuously distributed lag of equation 3.4. This
formulation leads to the analysis of a mixed differential-difference equation which
Goodwin reduced to a differential equation of the Liènard type and some of whose

solutions he analysed on an analogue computer. Techniques now exist to apply the method of averaging to the analysis of the limit cycle solution contained in differential-difference equations, see e.g. Migulin, Medvedev, Mustel and Parygin (1983), and so it is possible to analyse this case in the same way as we have analysed the continuously distributed lag.

3.4 A Saturation Type Nonlinear Accelerator

Here we assume the investment function is given by

$$B(Y, \dot{Y}) = v(Y)\ \dot{Y}, \tag{3.27}$$

with the accelerator coefficient $v(Y)$ having the form shown in figure 3.7. There we see that the accelerator coefficient is almost constant at $\bar{v}$ for levels of output around the equilibrium level $\bar{Y}$. But for large deviations of output above or below $\bar{Y}$ the accelerator coefficient drops quickly to a low value which is generally assumed to be zero in many theories of this type.

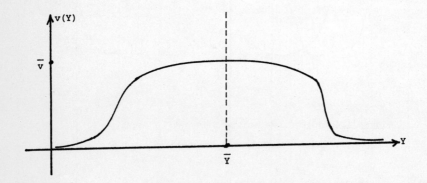

Figure 3.7 The nonlinear accelerator

The investment equation (3.27) encapsulates theories that see investment being choked off at abnormally high or abnormally low levels of economic activity. Such theories can be explained either from the demand side or the supply side. The value of the accelerator at the "normal" levels of economic activity, $\bar{v}$, is the accelerator of the standard linear theory.

From equation (3.8) we still have $\bar{Y} = G/s$. From (3.12) and (3.27) we find

$$e(y, \dot{y}) = (v(y + \bar{Y}) - \bar{v})\dot{y}, \tag{3.28}$$

so that the expression for $V(\rho)$ (equation (3.20)) reduces to

$$V(\rho) = \rho(H(\rho) - \bar{v}), \tag{3.29}$$

where

$$H(\rho) = \frac{1}{\pi} \int_0^{2\pi} v(\rho \cos \theta + \bar{Y}) \sin^2\theta \, d\theta. \tag{3.30}$$

The nonlinear differential equation (3.16) now takes the form

$$\dot{\rho} = \frac{\mu\rho}{2} (H(\rho) - (sT_i + T_0)). \tag{3.31}$$

We show in appendix 3.2 that the function H has the general shape shown in figure 3.8, where we also see the determination of the amplitude of the limit cycle at the intersection of $H(\rho)$ with the horizontal line $(sT_i + T_0)$.

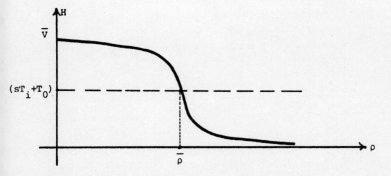

Figure 3.8 Determination of the amplitude in the nonlinear accelerater model

The resulting graph of $\dot{\rho}$ as a function of ρ is of exactly the same form as in figure 3.3 for the Goodwin nonlinear accelerator.

Here as in the Goodwin Model, we see the bifurcation nature of the model with $\rho = 0$ being the only stable equilibrum point for $\varepsilon < 0$ but a stable limit cycle of amplitude $\bar{\rho}$ appearing as ε increases through zero.

As in the Goodwin model the effect of the government stabilization policy expressed through equation (3.26) is to decrease the value of ε and hence to decrease the amplitude of the limit cycle. However in this model the fact that the function H decreases rapidly around $\rho = \bar{\rho}$, indicates that small changes in ε will not greatly affect the amplitude of the limit cycle.

It is also possible to investigate the relaxation oscillation limit of this model as T_i, $T_0 \to 0$, the details being similar to the corresponding calculation for the Goodwin model.

Appendix 3.1

We wish to obtain a sketch of the function H defined by equation (3.20).

Since $B(0) = 0$ it follows immediately that $H(0) = 0$.

In order to determine the limiting value of $H(\rho)$ as $\rho \to \infty$, we consider the integral in equation (3.21) over the intervals $(0, \pi)$ and $(\pi, 2\pi)$ where $B(\rho \sin \theta)$ is positive and negative respectively. Over each interval and at each value of θ the limiting value of $B(\rho \sin \theta)$ as $\theta \to \infty$ is respectively L and $-M$. Hence

$$\lim_{\rho \to \infty} H(\rho) = \frac{1}{\pi} \int_0^{2\pi} \lim_{\rho \to \infty} B(\rho \sin \theta) \sin \theta \, d\theta$$

$$= \frac{1}{\pi} \{ \int_0^{\pi} L \sin \theta \, d\theta + \int_{\pi}^{2\pi} (-M) \sin \theta \, d\theta \}$$

$$= 2(L + M)/\pi.$$

Other important properties of H are derived in the same way as was done for the function h in appendix 2.1. These properties are (i) $H'(\rho) > 0$ and (ii) $H''(\rho) < 0$. Finally note that

$$H'(0) = \frac{1}{\pi} \int_0^{2\pi} B'(0) \sin^2 \theta \, d\theta = v,$$

since $B'(0) = v$ by assumption.

Using all of the above assumptions we are able to sketch the function H as shown in figure 3.2.

Appendix 3.2

From equation (3.30) of the main text

$$H(\rho) = \frac{1}{\pi} \int_0^{2\pi} v(\rho \cos \psi + \bar{Y}) \sin^2 \psi \, d\psi.$$

First,

$$H(0) = \frac{\bar{v}}{\pi} \int_0^{2\pi} \cos^2 \psi \, d\psi = \bar{v}.$$

Also

$$\lim_{\rho \to \infty} H(\theta) = \frac{1}{\pi} \int_0^{2\pi} \lim_{\theta \to \infty} v \, (\rho \cos \psi + \bar{Y}) \sin^2 \psi \, d\psi = 0.$$

Next consider the derivative $H'(\rho)$ which is given by

$$H'(\rho) = \frac{1}{\pi} \int_0^{2\pi} v' \, (\rho \cos \psi + \bar{Y}) \cos \psi \sin^2 \psi \, d\psi.$$

By noting the sequence of implications

$$\cos \psi < (>) \, 0 \Rightarrow \rho \cos \psi + \bar{Y} < (>) \, \bar{Y} \Rightarrow v'(\rho \cos \psi + \bar{Y}) \geq (\leq) \, 0$$

we conclude that

$$H'(\rho) \leq 0.$$

Furthermore since $v'(\bar{Y}) \approx 0$ it follows from the expression for $H'(\rho)$ that $H'(0) \approx 0$.

Thus $H(\rho)$ must have the general shape shown in figure 3.8. There we see $H(\rho)$ coming out of $\bar{v}$ almost horizontally. Since $v'(Y)$ is almost zero, except over two relatively small intervals, $H'(\rho)$ will be close to zero except over a small interval of ρ. Hence $H(\rho)$ will decrease fairly rapidly over this same small interval of ρ, as shown in figure 3.8.

CHAPTER 4 **ANALYSIS OF THE EFFECTS OF TIME LAGS AND NONLINEARITIES IN MACROECONOMIC**
         MODELS INCORPORATING THE GOVERNMENT BUDGET RESTRAINT

4.1 **Introduction**

In the last chapter we demonstrated the two basic tools for the analysis of limit
cycle solutions to nonlinear differential equations, viz. the method of averaging and
the method of relaxation oscillations, on some of the traditional endogenous business
cycle theories. We saw there that this approach allows us to view such theories
within a unified mathematical framework, and we were thereby able to make a number of
simple extensions to these models. We were also able to gauge the effects of
traditional countercyclical policies on the amplitude of the cycle.

Since the construction of those endogenous cycle models and the development of the
theory of countercyclical policies a significant change in the conception of
macroeconomic modelling occured following the work of Christ (1968) and Blinder and
Solow (1973). These authors considered the implications of how the government
finances its fiscal and monetary policies, an aspect which had been overlooked in
macroeconomic theory up to that time but which turns out to be quite significant
given the size of government activity in modern industrial economies. There is now a
large literature on the government budget restraint and much of this is put in
perspective in the survey article of Rau (1985). A recurring theme in this
literature is the local stability or instability of the equilibrium under bond
financing. According to Rau the final verdict on this matter is that "..., it seems
safe to regard the possibility of stability under bond finance as a curiosum". Many
conclusions are drawn from this argument in particular that either bond financing of
the government budget is an inappropriate policy tool or that if in a model under
consideration there is some question as to the sign or magnitude of some parameter
then this could be determined from stability considerations.

An unstated assumption in the dynamic analysis of government budget restraint
(henceforth GBR) models is that the only possible solution concepts are those of
linear dynamical systems, the possibility of limit cycle solutions being thereby
excluded. As our discussion in the last chapter amply illustrated it is well
possible for a dynamic macroeconomic model to have a locally unstable equilibrium but
still exhibit stable limit cycle behaviour. In this chapter we shall consider a
basic version of the GBR model under bond financing and analyse the effects of two
elements which can yield limit cycle behaviour. These elements being a time lag in
the adjustment of the output market and the inclusion of one of the nonlinear

elements from the traditional endogenous cycle models discussed in the last chapter. In particular we incorporate the nonlinear investment mechanisms of the Kaldor model. However it is possible to incorporate any of the nonlinear mechanisms discussed in the last chapter into GBR models and carry out an analysis similar to that below. We should point out that a model similar to the one we analyse has been investigated by Schinasi (1982) who establishes the existence of limit cycle motion under both bond and money financing by use of the Poincaré-Bendixson theorem. Schinasi establishes his result by assuming the existence of a closed set on the boundary of which the vector field points inward. The analysis of Benassy (1984) shows some of the difficulties sinvolved in actually establishing the existence of such a set. Whilst analysis based on Poincaré-Bendixson theory can establish the existence of a limit cycle it is not able to shed any light on its stability or characteristics. That is the object of our approach and analysis.

4.2 Specification of the Model

Following the authors cited in section 4.1 we consider a model in which there is a market for a homogeneous good whose level of output is denoted by Y. The model also contains a money market where the demand for money depends upon output Y, the nominal rate of interest r and total wealth W. If B represents the number of outstanding government bonds paying \$1 per year in perpetuity, then wealth is measured by $W = M + B/r$. Money demand is a function of Y, r and W. Using M to denote the supply of money at any given moment, the condition for equilibrium of the money market may be written

$$M = L_1 Y + L_2 r + L_3 (M + B/r). \qquad (4.1)$$

We make the standard assumptions that $L_1 > 0$, $L_2 < 0$ and $0 < L_3 < 1$. Equation (4.1) implicitly defines the nominal interest rate r as a function of Y, B and M, which we write as

$$r = r(Y, B, M). \qquad (4.2)$$

Setting $p = L_3 B/r^2 - L_2 > 0$, we find that the partial derivatives of r are given by

$$r_1 = L_1/p > 0, \quad r_2 = L_3/rp > 0 \text{ and } r_3 = -(1 - L_3)/p < 0. \qquad (4.3)$$

Turning now to the output market, consumption demand may be written as

$$C = c_1(1 - \tau)(Y + B) + c_2(M + B/\tau), \tag{4.4}$$

where c_1 $(0<c_1<1)$ is the propensity to consume from disposable income, c_2 $(0<c_2<1)$ is the propensity to consume from wealth, and τ $(0<\tau<1)$ is the tax rate.

Here disposable income is the sum of output Y and the interest payments on the stock of outstanding government bonds held by consumers.
Investment demand may be written as

$$I = V(Y) + I_2 \tau \tag{4.5}$$

where $V(Y)$ is a function which shall be specified shortly. We make the standard assumptions that $dV(Y)/dY = I_1 > 0$ and $I_2 < 0$. The nonlinear element that we introduce into the model is Kaldor's (1940) nonlinear investment mechanism. Kaldor introduced this investment function in order to develop an endogenous cycle model. The fundamental assumption is that I_1, the marginal rate of investment with respect to output, is relatively high around the equilibrium value of output (to be determined below) and relatively low far from this equilibrium value.

In order to capture the influence of some of the traditional countercyclical fiscal policies we assume that the demands of the government sector are of the form

$$G = \bar{G} + \omega \dot{Y}. \tag{4.6}$$

where $\bar{G}$ is some base level of government spending and ω is a constant. Using the classification of Turnovsky (1977) this is a Phillips derivative stabilization policy. For $\omega > 0$, equation (4.6) states that government spending rises above the base level when output is increasing (i.e. during a boom) and falls below the base level when output is declining (i.e. during a recession). When $\omega < 0$, the government spending is reversed, namely output falls below the base level during a boom and rises above this level during a recession. As a practical consideration ω would normally be a fraction so we shall assume $|\omega| < 1$.

Aggregate demand for output is given by

$$Z = C + I + G,$$
or
$$Z = F(Y, B, M) + \omega \dot{Y}, \tag{4.7}$$

where

$$F(Y,B,M) = c_1(1-\tau)(Y+B) + c_2(M-L_1Y-L_2r)/L_3 + V(Y) + I_2r + \bar{G}. \qquad (4.8)$$

We shall assume that the supply of output adjusts sluggishly to excess demand, so that the evolution of output Y conforms to the differential equation

$$\dot{Y} = \gamma(Z - Y), \qquad (4.9)$$

where γ is a positive constant. After substituting (4.7) into (4.9), we find that the differential equation for Y reduces to

$$\dot{Y} = \gamma'[F(Y,B,M) - Y], \qquad (4.10)$$

where $\gamma' = \gamma/(1 - \gamma\omega)$.

The government increases the money stock and issues or retires bonds at a rate sufficient to finance its budget deficit. Thus we have the government budget restraint

$$\dot{M} + \frac{\dot{B}}{r} = \bar{G} + \omega\dot{Y} - \tau Y + (1 - \tau)B, \qquad (4.11)$$

where the right hand side defines the government's budget deficit consisting of the difference between government outlays, $\bar{G} + \omega\dot{Y} + B$, and government receipts, $\tau(Y + B)$, from taxation of disposable income. The pair of differential equations (4.10) and (4.11) determines the evolution of Y, B and M once the 'mix' of money and bond financing is set.

We shall consider a pure bond financing regime so that $\dot{M} = 0$, in which case equation (4.11) reduces to

$$\frac{\dot{B}}{r} = \bar{G} + \omega\dot{Y} - \tau Y + (1 - \tau)B. \qquad (4.12)$$

The equilibrium values $(\bar{Y}, \bar{B})$ are obtained by setting $\dot{Y} = \dot{B} = 0$ in (4.10-4.12) and solving the resulting pair of algebraic equations.

The equations determining the equilibrium are (from 4.10)

$$Y = F(Y,B,M), \qquad (4.13)$$

and (from 4.12)

$$Y = (\bar{G} + (1-\tau)B)/\tau. \tag{4.14}$$

Equation (4.14) represents a straight line of slope $(1-\tau)/\tau$, however in order to obtain an idea of the shape of the function represented by equation (4.13) we need to calculate the partial derivative $\partial Y/\partial B$. Differentiating (4.13) implicitly we find that

$$\partial Y/\partial B = \beta/\varphi, \tag{4.15}$$

where

$$\varphi = 1 - c_1(1 - \tau) - I_1 - I_2 r_1 + c_2(L_1 + L_2 r_1)/L_3, \tag{4.16a}$$

$$\beta = c_1(1 - \tau) + I_2 r_2 - c_2 L_2 r_2/L_3, \tag{4.16b}$$

and, for later use we also define

$$\delta = I_2 r_3 + c_2(1 - L_2 r_3)/L_3. \tag{4.16c}$$

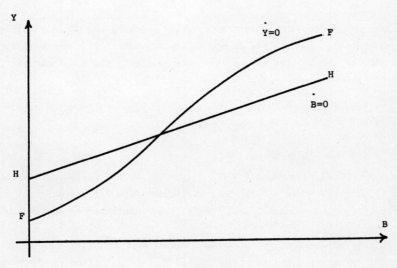

Figure 4.1

The assumed behaviour of $I_1(Y)$ around the equilibrium point leads to the graph of equation 4.13 which is labelled FF in figure 4.1. This graph has been drawn under the assumption $\beta > 0$ and details are given in appendix 4.2. It is also pointed out in that appendix that a number of other cases are possible. We choose to analyse solely the case represented in figure 4.1 in order to illustrate how the ideas being presented in this thesis may be applied to a proper dynamic analysis of government budget restraint models. A complete understanding of the model discussed in this chapter would require a detailed analysis of all the other cases as well. This would require a separate thesis in its own right and would take us beyond the goal we have set ourselves for the present chapter.

We also locate on figure 4.1 the straight line HH which represents the set of points
$$\dot{B} = 0$$

Setting $y = Y - \bar{Y}$ and $b = B - \bar{B}$, and expanding the right hand sides of equations (4.10) and (4.12) around the equilibrium point we are led to consider the pair of differential equations

$$\dot{y} = -\gamma'\varphi \, y + \gamma'\beta b, \tag{4.17}$$

and

$$\frac{\dot{b}}{r} = \omega y - ry + (1 - r)b. \tag{4.18}$$

We stress that the differential system (4.17-18) contains the nonlinear investment function in the variable φ which has as one of its arguments, I_1, the marginal rate of investment out of income. We now specify more precisely the nonlinearity in I_1 by defining

$$I_1 = \begin{cases} \bar{I}_1, & |y| < |y_0| \\ \hat{I}_1, & |y| > |y_0| \end{cases} \tag{4.19}$$

where y_0 is some fixed value and $0 < \hat{I}_1 < \bar{I}_1 < 1$. In the followong discussion we choose units of output so that $y_0 = 1$. This particular form for the marginal rate of investment out of income is drawn from Kaldor's (1940) nonlinear investment function.

In Kaldor's original discussion the nonlinear investment function was an S shaped function in the I-Y plane. The function implied by the definition of I_1 in equation (4.19) is a piece-wise linear idealization of the S shaped function, as illustrated in figure 4.2. Our purpose in introducing this idealization is to illustrate another useful technique for analysing the differential equation which occurs in the application of the method of averaging. The analysis of the nonlinear element could of course also be performed by the same general approach as in the last chapter.

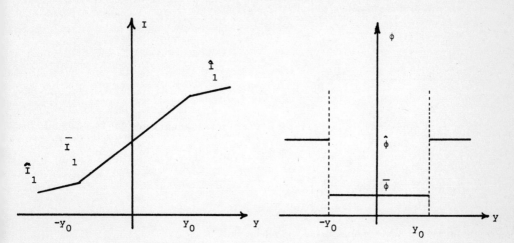

Figure 4.2 Piece-wise linear investment function   Figure 4.3 Nonlinearity in ϕ

For the purposes of our analysis, the important impact of the nonlinear marginal rate of investment is on the coefficient φ, which assumes the form shown in Figure 4.3, where

$$\hat{\varphi} = 1 - c_1(1 - \tau) - \hat{I}_1 - I_2 r_1 + c_2(L_1 + L_2 r_1)/L_3, \tag{4.20a}$$

and

$$\bar{\varphi} = 1 - c_1(1 - \tau) - \bar{I}_1 - I_2 r_1 + c_2(L_1 + L_2 r_1)/L_3. \tag{4.20b}$$

Letting $\bar{\epsilon} = \hat{\psi} - \bar{\psi}$ and defining the following function:

$$\epsilon(y) = \begin{cases} 0, & |y| < 1, \\[2mm] -\bar{\epsilon}, & |y| > 1, \end{cases} \tag{4.21}$$

the differential equation (4.17) for y may be written as

$$\dot{y} = -\gamma'\bar{\varphi}y + \gamma'\beta b + \gamma'y\epsilon(y). \tag{4.22}$$

The dynamics of the income-expenditure model, with the government deficit financed by bond issues, is given by the pair of differential equations (4.22) and (4.18). The possibility of limit cycle motion in this model arises through the nonlinear form of the coefficient φ. As we shall see below, the relationship of $\bar{\varphi}$ to $\hat{\varphi}$ may cause the system to move away from the origin if (y, b) are small, but to move towards the origin for (y, b) large. For further clarification, we now turn to a dynamic analysis of the differential equation in y and b.

4.3 **Dynamic Behaviour of the Model**

After some rearrangement, the pair of differential equations (4.14, 18) may be written in matrix form as

$$
\begin{bmatrix} \dot{y} \\ \dot{b} \end{bmatrix} = A \begin{bmatrix} y \\ b \end{bmatrix} + \gamma' y \epsilon(y) \begin{bmatrix} 1 \\ \omega \end{bmatrix}
\tag{4.23}
$$

where the matrix A has components a_{ij} given by

$$
a_{11} = -\gamma'\bar{\varphi} \; , \; a_{12} = \gamma'\beta, \; a_{21} = -r(\tau + \omega\gamma'\bar{\varphi}), \; \text{and} \; a_{22} = r(\omega\gamma'\beta + 1 - \tau).
\tag{4.24}
$$

Straightforward calculations yield

$$
\det(A) = r\gamma'\bar{\varphi}\tau(\beta/\bar{\varphi} - (1 - \tau)/\tau)
\tag{4.25}
$$

and

$$
\mathrm{tr}(A) = -\gamma'(\bar{\varphi} - r\omega\beta) + r(1 - \tau).
\tag{4.26}
$$

We assume that the values of γ and ω are such that $\gamma' > 0$. Hence, det (A) > 0 when

$$
\beta/\bar{\varphi} > (1 - \tau)/\tau
\tag{4.27}
$$

in which case the origin of the (y, b) axes is either a source or a sink, thereby excluding saddle point behaviour. Henceforth, we shall assume that (4.27) holds and note that it is in fact the condition found by Blinder-Solow for bond financing to be stable in a model where the output market clears instantaneously. So we are considering the case which is most favourable for bond financing and find that nevertheless local stability turns to local instability due to nonlinear effects and subsequently limit cycle motion occurs.

The interesting dynamic features of the model arise from consideration of tr(A).

Assuming $\bar{\varphi} > r\omega\beta$, we see that tr(A) is a monotonically decreasing function of γ' (which in turn is an increasing function of γ), with tr(A) > 0 at $\gamma' = 0$. Thus there is a critical value of γ', which we denote by γ'_c, at which tr(A) = 0. If we assume that the speed of adjustment in the output market is such that $\gamma' < \gamma'_c$, then tr(A) > 0 and the equilibrium point y = b = 0 is locally unstable. However, as y and b move away from the equilibrium the nonlinear investment mechanism comes into play, and $\bar{\varphi}$ is replaced by $\hat{\varphi}$ in tr(A). This jump in the coefficient φ leads to a decline in the value of tr(A).

If the parameters of the model are such that tr(A) changes from positive to negative as a result of the change in the coefficient φ, then far from equilibrium the motion of y and b is governed by a linear differential equation whose coefficient matrix has negative eigenvalues. Hence, far from equilibrium the motion of y and b is back towards the origin. The balancing of these two tendencies leads to stable limit cycle motion of y and b. The sign switching of tr(A) is illustrated in Figure 4.4.

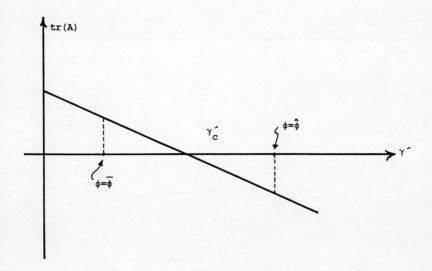

Figure 4.4

We recall that the eigenvalues of the matrix A are given by

$$\lambda = \{ tr(A) \pm \sqrt{[tr(A)^2 - 4 \det(A)]} \}/2 = u \pm iv. \qquad (4.28)$$

Now at $\gamma' = \gamma'_c$, tr(A) = 0 and hence the eigenvalues are pure complex. Since we are assuming γ' is close to γ'_c, the eigenvalues will be complex with a small real part. Thus the motion away from the origin will be cyclical.

Applying the method of averaging we find a first approximation to the amplitude of the limit cycle satisfies the differential equation

$$\dot{\rho} = u\rho + f(\rho),\qquad(4.29)$$

where $u = tr(A)/2$ and, $f(\rho) = \rho h(\rho)$ with

$$h(\rho) = \frac{\gamma'}{2\pi}\int_0^{2\pi} \epsilon(\rho \sin \theta)(\sin^2\theta + \omega \sin \theta \cos \theta)d\theta.\qquad(4.30)$$

It is more convenient to express the equation (4.29) in the form

$$\dot{\rho} = \rho(u + h(\rho)).\qquad(4.31)$$

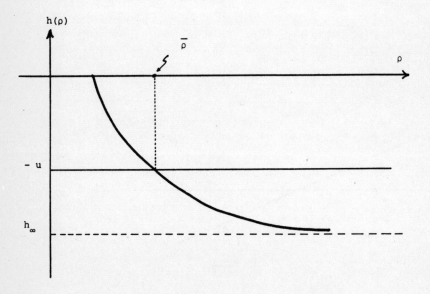

Figure 4.5 The function h and the determination of $\bar{\rho}$

Using the piece-wise linear representation of $\epsilon(y)$ we are able to calculate an explicit form for $h(\rho)$. This is done in appendix 4.1 and we are able to deduce that the general shape of h is as displayed in figure 4.5. The graphical determination of $\bar{\rho}$ is also displayed, and we see that two cases are possible depending on

(i) $u > -\gamma'\bar{\epsilon}(1-\omega/2) = h_\infty$, and (ii) $u < h_\infty$. Case (i) yields a limit cycle at $\bar{\rho}$, which is stable since $\dot{\rho} > 0 \ (< 0)$ for $\rho < \bar{\rho} \ (> \bar{\rho})$, while case (ii) yields steady motion away from the origin. The graph of $\dot{\rho}$ as a function of ρ for each case is displayed in figure (4.6).

In case (ii) the system is totally unstable with the time paths for y and b exploding to infinity. In order to bound this motion the present model would have to be placed in the context of a more general model taking account of other nonlinear constraints in both the goods and money markets (e.g. output constraints as well as credit constraints) and also taking account of prices and price expectations.

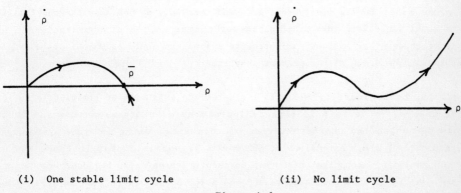

(i) One stable limit cycle   (ii) No limit cycle

<u>Figure 4.6</u>

Our interest concentrates on the stable limit cycle, $\bar{\rho}$, arising from the intersection of the horizontal line -u with the negatively sloping portion of the function h. The effect of parametric changes on the amplitude of the cycle is determined by gauging their effect on u and on the horizontal asymptote, h_∞, of the function h. The effect of some parametric changes is unambiguous, for example, an increase in the tax rate, τ, leads to a lower value of u and hence to a decrease in the amplitude of the limit cycle. Similarly any change which "ceteris paribus" increases $\bar{\varphi}$ increases the amplitude of the cycle since

$$\partial u/\partial\bar{\varphi} = -\gamma'/2 < 0 \quad \text{and} \quad \partial h_\infty/\partial\bar{\varphi} = \gamma'(1-\omega/2) > 0$$

Note that in obtaining the signs of these partial derivatives we have assumed $\bar{\varphi} > r\omega\beta$ which is not unreasonable given that ω is usually much smaller than unity.
However the effect of the parametric change which is probably most important from the point of view of the policy maker, namely that of the contracyclical spending policy, measured by changes in ω, remains ambiguous. This is so since

$$\partial h_\alpha/\partial\omega = - \bar{\epsilon}(1-\omega/2) \ \partial\gamma'/\partial\omega + \gamma'\bar{\epsilon} > 0,$$

which tends to increase the amplitude of the cycle, whilst

$$\partial u/\partial\omega = \{ \ -(\bar{\varphi} - r\omega\beta) \ \partial\gamma'/\partial\omega + \gamma'r\beta \ \}/2 > 0,$$

which tends to decrease the amplitude of the cycle. Thus the effectiveness of the contracyclical spending policy is very dependent upon the estimated values of the model at hand. This would indicate that the use of contracyclical policies is a far more subtle matter than many of its proponents realise.

In the foregoing analysis we have considered a particular range of parameter values, namely $0 < \gamma' < \gamma_c'$, $\bar{\varphi} > r\omega\beta$ and equation (4.27). We have done this in order to analyse the model in its limit cycle mode and certainly do not deny the possibility that the model would fall into other parameter ranges as the economy evolves. The analysis of these other motions would require a separate analysis which, again, would take us beyond the scope of the present chapter.

The analysis of Schinasi (1982) also indicates the existence of limit cycle motion when the government deficit is financed purely by monetary expansion and it is possible to analse the characteristics of this cycle using the same approach as above. A number of other extensions of GBR models is possible, for instance any of the other nonlinear mechanisms discussed in chapter three could be incorporated into the framework. It is also possible to analyse price movements in such models along the lines of Infante and Stein (1980), indeed such an analysis would seem most appropriate since their linear analysis indicates the existence of cyclical motion.

Appendix 4.1

Rewriting equation (4.26) we have

$$h(\rho) = \frac{\gamma'}{2\pi} \int_0^{2\pi} \epsilon(\rho \sin \theta)(\sin^2\theta + \omega \sin \theta \cos \theta)d\theta.$$

Defining $\xi = \arcsin(1/\rho)$ and applying the defintion (4.17) for $\epsilon(\rho \sin \theta)$ we have

$$\epsilon(\rho \sin \theta) = \begin{cases} 0 & \text{for} \quad \theta \in \Omega_0, \\ -\epsilon & \text{for} \quad \theta \in \Omega_1, \end{cases}$$

where the sets Ω_0, Ω_1 are defined by

$$\Omega_0 = (0, \xi) \cup (\pi - \xi, \pi + \xi) \cup (2\pi - \xi, 2\pi),$$

and

$$\Omega_1 = (\xi, \pi - \xi) \cup (\pi + \xi, 2\pi - \xi).$$

These sets are easily obtained from a consideration of the graph of $\rho \sin \theta$.

Hence

$$\frac{2\pi}{\gamma'}h(\rho) = \int_{\xi}^{\pi-\xi} (-\bar{\epsilon})(\sin^2\theta + \omega\sin\theta\cos\theta)d\theta + \int_{\pi+\xi}^{2\pi-\xi} (-\bar{\epsilon})(\sin^2\theta + \omega\sin\theta\cos\theta)d\theta$$

Using the results

$$\int \sin^2\theta \, d\theta = \frac{\theta}{2} - \frac{1}{2} \sin \theta \cos \theta \,,$$

and

$$\int \sin \theta \cos \theta \, d\theta = \frac{1}{2} \sin^2\theta - \frac{1}{4} \,,$$

we find that

$$\int_{\xi}^{\pi-\xi} \sin^2\theta \, d\theta + \int_{\pi+\xi}^{2\pi-\xi} \sin^2\theta \, d\theta = \left[\frac{\theta}{2} - \frac{\sin\theta\cos\theta}{2}\right]_{\xi}^{\pi-\xi} + \left[\frac{\theta}{2} - \frac{\sin\theta\cos\theta}{2}\right]_{\pi+\xi}^{2\pi-\xi}$$

$$= \pi - 2\xi + 2 \sin \xi \cos \xi,$$

and

$$\int_{\xi}^{\pi-\xi} \sin\theta \, \cos\theta \, d\theta + \int_{\pi+\xi}^{2\pi-\xi} \sin\theta \, \cos\theta \, d\theta = 0.$$

Hence

$$h(\rho) = -\frac{\gamma'\bar{\epsilon}}{2\pi}\left[\pi - 2\xi + 2\sin\xi\,\cos\xi\right].$$

To obtain the graph of this function we first observe that as ρ varies from 1 to ∞, ξ varies from $\pi/2$ to 0. The function

$$H(\xi) = \pi - 2\xi + \sin 2\xi,$$

satisfies $H(0) = (1 - \omega/2)\pi$ and $H(\pi/2) = 0$. Multiplying H by the factor $-\gamma'\bar{\epsilon}/2\pi$ to obtain the function h and transforming to the independent variable ρ we obtain the graph shown in figure 4.5.

Appendix 4.2

The assumption that $I_1(Y)$ is relatively high around $\bar{Y}$ and relatively low away from $\bar{Y}$ means that β/ψ as a function of Y must have one of the general shapes shown in figure 4.7. Case (a) corresponds to $\varphi > 0$ for all Y, case (b) arises when φ crosses the Y axis (which it must do at two points) and case (c) arises when $\varphi < 0$ for all Y. All of these cases are drawn under the assumption $\beta > 0$, the $\beta < 0$ cases are simply the mirror images of those in the horizontal axis. We can next use the slope information contained in figure 4.7 to to obtain the qualitative features of Y $-$ F(Y,B,M) = 0. In this manner we have obtained figure 4.8, each subcase corresponding to the equivalent subcase in figure 4.7. The case we analyse in chapter 4 is case (a) in the situation when $\bar{G}$ is such that the intercept with the vertical axis is below the intercept of B = 0 with the same axis.

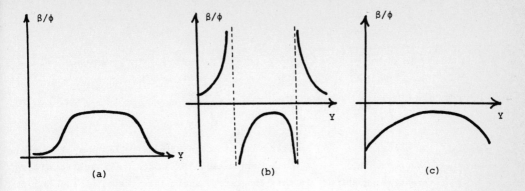

Figure 4.7

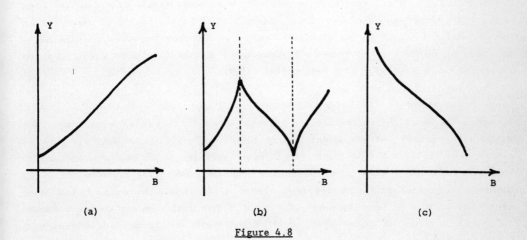

Figure 4.8

CHAPTER 5   <u>LIMIT CYCLES IN HIGHER DIMENSIONS - THE EFFECT OF TIME LAGS ON GOODWIN'S</u>
<u>MODEL OF CYCLICAL GROWTH</u>

5.1 <u>Introduction</u>

In the last two chapters we have applied some of the nonlinear techniques of chapter
two to various macroeconomic models which mathematically reduce to a system of two
nonlinear differential equations. In this chapter we shall illustrate the analysis of
a three dimensional nonlinear system by use of the centre manifold concepts discussed
in section 2.7. A convenient model on which to illustrate these concepts is Goodwin's
(1967) model of cyclical growth. This model for some considerable time received scant
attention in the economics literature, apart from the contribution of Desai (1973).
However recent interest in theories of economic cycles has led to a resurgence of
activity on Goodwin's model, see e.g. Goodwin et al., (1984), Blatt (1983), van der
Ploeg (1983), Medio (1979), and Vellupillai (1979).

Goodwin expressed the evolution of the share of wages and employment in a growing
economy in terms of the Lotka-Volterra predator-prey differential equations. The
main characteristic of the model is that the distributive shares move along closed
cycles whose amplitudes depend upon the initial conditions. From the mathematical
point of view the system of differential equations underlying the model, although
nonlinear, is conservative and displays closed orbits with the equilibrium being
neutrally stable.   From the point of view of a theory of economic cycles the model
remains an important schematic model of the trade cycle and is an improvement over
linear models in that the cycle persists as parameters of the model change
arbitrarily. However the model has the disadvantage that arbitrarily small
perturbations in the initial conditions yield a cycle of different amplitude. As we
have emphasised in earlier chapters a more satisfactory theory of economic cycles
would have the amplitude depending only on the structure of the model rather than on
the initial conditions. Indeed the Goodwin model is structurally unstable in that
any slight arbitrary perturbation to its structure (i.e. by adding arbitrarily small
additional terms to the right-hand side of the differential system governing the
model) destroys the stable neutrality of its equilibrium. The stability of the
Goodwin model (and a slight extension of it) has been extensively discussed by
Vellupillai.

If the Goodwin model is to provide a satisfactory model of economic cycles changes
must be made to its mathematical structure so that the governing differential
equations exhibit stable limit cycle behaviour. Medio (1979) has already done some

analysis of such changes relying largely on Kolmogoroff's (1931) generalization of Volterra's (1931) original analysis. Our aim here is to consider a mechanism that can cause the Goodwin model to yield stable limit cycles. The basic mechanism is the introduction of time lags which interact with the nonlinearities of the model to break the family of closed cycles to yield instead a stable limit cycle. Our contribution is intended to add to an understanding of the dynamic behaviour of the Goodwin model as well as illustrate the use of centre manifold theory. Our techniques are inspired by recent advances in the mathematical analysis of predator-prey systems; see e.g. Freedman and Waltman (1975) for a technical discussion and May (1976b) for a more discursive account.

5.2 **The Goodwin Model with a Time-Lag**

In this section we shall introduce a time lag into the wage formation mechanism of the Goodwin model. In deriving the equations of the model we shall follow as closely as possible Goodwin's original notation.

Homogeneous output is denoted by q and capital stock by k. The wage rate is w and labour productivity is a where $\dot{a}/a = \alpha$, a constant and ˙ denotes differentiation with respect to time. We shall make the standard assumption that the capital-output ratio, σ, is a constant. The labour supply, n, is assumed to grow at the constant rate β, i.e., $\dot{n}/n = \beta$. The workers' share of product is u = w/a. The level of employment is l = q/a and the employment rate is v = l/n.

Goodwin assumed that the rate of wage change was a positive function of the employment rate, i.e.,

$$\frac{\dot{w}}{w} = -\gamma + \rho v \quad (\gamma > 0, \ \rho > 0). \tag{5.1}$$

We shall generalize equation (5.1) by assuming that $\dot{w}/w$ is a positive function of a weighted index of the employment rate over past periods. i.e., we replace (5.1) by

$$\frac{\dot{w}}{w} = -\gamma + \rho x, \tag{5.2}$$

where

$$x(t) = \int_{-\infty}^{t} \frac{e^{-(t-s)/T}}{T} v(s)ds. \tag{5.3}$$

Here x(t) is a continuously distributed weighted average of all past employment rates, with the weighting function being a declining exponential. The parameter T is best thought of as the mean time lag and assigns more (T large) or less (T small) weight to past employment rates; in the limit $T \to 0$, it can be shown that $x(t) = v(t)$. It would probably be more realistic to take the continuously distributed weighted average over a finite interval, say $[t, t - \tau]$ for τ fixed, or to consider a discrete weighted average. However both of these more realistic weighting schemes would lead to a model expressed in terms of a mixed differential-difference equation whose analysis would be extremely complex, if not impossible, in the nonlinear framework of the Goodwin model. We feel that (5.3) is a practical compromise; it enables us to capture the broad qualitative features of time lags in the wage equation and leads to a differential system which is (just) mathematically tractable.

The basic idea behind equation (5.2), that wages adjust sluggishly to excess supply of labour goes back at least to Keynes (1936, see e.g. Chapter 19) and is still considered an important element in theories of the business cycle; see Zarnowitz (1985).

Before proceeding we note from differentiation of equation (5.3) that x satisfies the differential equation

$$\dot{x} = (v - x)/T. \tag{5.4}$$

We may now derive the differential equations satisfied by the employment rate v and the worker's share of product u.

Differentiating logarithmically $v = l/n$ and $l = q/a$ we find that

$$\frac{\dot{v}}{v} = \frac{\dot{l}}{l} - \frac{\dot{n}}{n} = \frac{\dot{q}}{q} - \frac{\dot{a}}{a} - \frac{\dot{n}}{n} = \frac{\dot{q}}{q} - (\alpha + \beta). \tag{5.5}$$

From the assumption that all profits are invested we have that

$$\dot{k} = (1 - u)q, \tag{5.6}$$

and since $\sigma = k/q$, we also have

$$\frac{\dot{q}}{q} = \frac{\dot{k}}{k} = \frac{(1 - u)}{\sigma}. \tag{5.7}$$

Substituting (5.7) into (5.5) we have the first differential equation of the Goodwin model, viz.

$$\dot{v} = [(\frac{1}{\sigma} - (\alpha + \beta)) - \frac{1}{\sigma} u]v. \tag{5.8}$$

From the defining relationship $u = w/a$ and equation (5.2) we obtain the second equation

$$\dot{u} = [-(\alpha + \gamma) + \rho x] u, \tag{5.9}$$

the system is completed by the differential equation for x, i.e. equation (5.4), which we reproduce:-

$$\dot{x} = (v - x)/T .$$ (5.4)

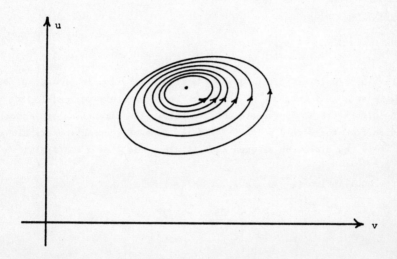

Figure 5.1 The closed cycles of the standard Goodwin model when T = 0.

The Goodwin model now consists of the three differential equations for v, u and x. When T = 0, so that there is no lag in the wage rate equation, equation (5.4) collapses to x = v and equations (5.8) and (5.9) reduce to the standard 2-dimensional Goodwin model, which displays a family of closed cycles as shown in figure 5.1.

5.3 Local Stability Analysis

The differential system governing the model has two equilibrium points, namely,

$$\bar{v} = \bar{x} = 0, \ \bar{u} = 0,$$ (5.10)

and

$$v^* = x^* = (\alpha + \gamma)/\rho, \ u^* = 1 - \sigma(\alpha + \beta).$$ (5.11)

It is conventional to assume u* > 0. In order to determine the local stability properties of each equilibrium point we need to consider the Jacobian matrix of the differential system (5.4), (5.8) and (5.9), evaluated at each equilibrium. We shall denote these Jacobian matrices by $\bar{J}$ and J^* respectively.

First consider the equilibrium at the origin. We readily find that

$$
\bar{J} = \begin{bmatrix} u^*/\sigma & 0 & 0 \\ 0 & -v^*\rho & 0 \\ 1/T & 0 & -1/T \end{bmatrix} ,
\tag{5.12}
$$

which has eigenvalues $(u^*/\sigma, -v^*\rho, -1/T)$ whose sign distribution is (+, -, -). Hence the origin is a saddle point, as is the case for Goodwin's original model. By calculating the eigenvectors of $\bar{J}$ we are able to obtain the directions of contraction to and expansion from the saddle point. The directions of contraction are along the u and x axes, while the direction of expansion is along the line $v = x(1 + Tu^*/\sigma)$ in the plane u = 0.
Now consider the equilibrium (v^*, u^*, x^*), at which

$$
J^* = \begin{bmatrix} 0 & -v^*/\sigma & 0 \\ 0 & 0 & \rho u^* \\ 1/T & 0 & -1/T \end{bmatrix} .
\tag{5.13}
$$

The eigenvalues of J^* are the roots of the cubic equation

$$
T \lambda^3 + \lambda^2 + \Omega^2 = 0 ,
\tag{5.14}
$$
where $\Omega^2 = \rho u^* v^*/\sigma$.

Note that in the unlagged model, when T = 0, (5.14) reduces to a quadratic equation with roots $\lambda = \pm i\Omega$, hence reproducing (locally) the closed orbits of the standard Goodwin model. Our interest is in the case T > 0, and we shall show that the model exhibits limit cycle behaviour in this case.

We show in appendix 5.1 that the roots of the cubic (5.14) have the properties that (a) there is one negative real root which $\to -\infty$ as $T \to 0$, (b) there is a pair of complex roots whose real part, denoted by R(T), is positive for all T > 0 and has the properties R(0) = 0, R'(0) > 0. The property (b) allow us to invoke the Hopf bifurcation theorem to demonstrate that a limit cycle emerges as T passes through 0. What requires further analysis is to determine whether the limit cycle exists for T < 0 or for T > 0 (according to bifurcation theory a limit cycle for both T < 0 and T > 0 is not possible).

5.4 Approximation of the Limit Cycle

A complete qualitative analysis of the limit cycle solutions of the three nonlinear differential equations (5.4), (5.8) and (5.9) is beyond the reach of current mathematical techniques. However we are able to obtain a picture of the behaviour when T is small. The crucial observation which enables us to analyse this case is that, from the differential equation (5.4), when T is small and > 0, $\dot{x}$ is large except in a neighbourhood of the plane v = x. Furthermore, it is clear from equation (5.4) that motion is towards this neighbourhood. The situation is illustrated in figure 5.2, where we see that motion will be towards a manifold whose equation (as yet to be determined) is denoted by

$$x = h(u, v) , \qquad\qquad (5.15)$$

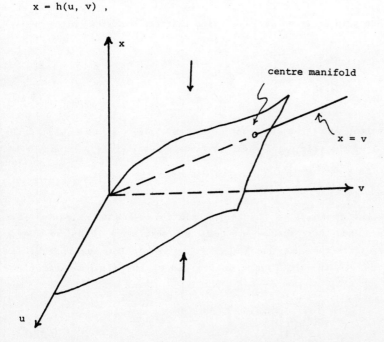

Figure 5.2 Motion towards the centre manifold

and which is in a neighbourhood of the plane x = v. This manifold, as we have pointed out in section 2.7, is known as the centre-manifold. The dynamics of the system are qualitatively determined by the dynamics on the centre-manifold, to which, as we have pointed out, all trajectories are tending. The aim of our analysis is therefore to determine the dynamic behaviour on the centre-manifold. We already know that in the limit T = 0 the centre-manifold becomes the plane x = v and that all trajectories on this manifold are the familiar closed curves of the original Goodwin model. Guckenheimer and Holmes (1983) outline procedures for approximating the function h, the essence of which is to seek its Taylor expansion and to determine the Taylor coefficients in such a way that the differential equations (5.4), (5.8) and (5.9) remain consistent with such an expansion. In appendix 5.2 we find that up to quadratic terms the centre-manifold is given by

$$x = a(1 + \epsilon u)v, \tag{5.16}$$

where

$$a = 1/(1 + Tu^*/\sigma) \text{ and } \epsilon = T/(\sigma + T(u^* - \sigma\rho v^*)). \tag{5.17}$$

Note that as $T \to 0$ we have $a \to 1$ and $\epsilon \to 0$, as we would expect from our above discussion.

Using (5.16) to replace x in equation (5.9), we find that the dynamics on the centre-manifold are given by

$$\dot{v} = \frac{1}{\sigma} (u^* - u)v , \tag{5.18a}$$

$$\dot{u} = \rho(-v^* + av)u + \rho\epsilon au^2 v . \tag{5.18b}$$

Whilst the equilibrium $(\tilde{u}, \tilde{v})$ of the differential system (5.18) is not equal to the equilibrium (u^*, v^*) of the original system, we find by putting $\dot{u} = \dot{v} = 0$ in (5.18) that

$$\tilde{u} = u^*, \quad \tilde{v} = v^* + O(T^2) . \tag{5.19}$$

In order to analyse the dynamics on the centre manifold we shall need to use approximating arguments, and those that we use below are accurate to O(T), so that to this order of accuracy it is the case that $(\tilde{u}, \tilde{v}) = (u^*, v^*)$. The local stability properties of the equilibrium (u, v) are determined by the eigenvalues of the Jacobian matrix

$$J = \begin{bmatrix} 0 & - v^*/\sigma \\ \rho au^*(1 + \epsilon u^*) & \epsilon\rho au^* v^* \end{bmatrix} , \tag{5.20}$$

which reduces to the Jacobian matrix J^* when $a = 1$ and $\epsilon = 0$. Setting $p = \rho au^* v^*/2$ and $\eta^2 = 2(1 + \epsilon u^*)/\sigma p$ we find that the eigenvalues of J are given by

$$\lambda = \epsilon p \pm ip \sqrt{(\eta^2 - \epsilon^2)} \approx \epsilon p \pm i\omega , \tag{5.21}$$

which are complex since we are assuming ϵ is small. Since $p > 0$ and $\epsilon > 0$, equation (5.21) indicates that (u^*, v^*) is locally unstable, with trajectories spiralling outwards. This local behaviour indicates the possibility of a limit cycle, to whose analysis we now turn.

We indicated in section 2.5 that we would use the Goodwin model to illustrate the more standard way of applying the method of averaging to approximate limit cycles rather than the approach we have adopted in chapters three and four. In order to analyse the limit cycle solution of equation (5.18) in this way we use the eigenvectors of J to transform from (u, v) to a new set of so called canonical coordinates (X, Y) which are centred at (u^*, v^*) and in which the limit cycle becomes a circle; see figure 5.3. In fact,

$$X = u - u^*, \tag{5.22a}$$

$$Y = \frac{-\sigma\omega}{u^*} (v - v^*) - \frac{\epsilon\sigma p}{v^*} (u - u^*), \tag{5.22b}$$

and in terms of these coordinates the differential system (5.18) reduces to

$$\begin{bmatrix} \dot{X} \\ \dot{Y} \end{bmatrix} = \begin{bmatrix} \epsilon p & \omega \\ -\omega & \epsilon p \end{bmatrix} \begin{bmatrix} X \\ Y \end{bmatrix} + \begin{bmatrix} f_1(X, Y) \\ f_2(X, Y) \end{bmatrix}, \tag{5.23}$$

where the nonlinear terms f_1, f_2 are of quadratic and cubic order in X and Y and are defined in appendix 5.3. The spiralling motion of the differential system (5.23) is analysed by transforming to polar coordinates $X = r \cos \theta$, $Y = r \sin \theta$ and applying the method of averaging as outlined in section 2.5 to (5.23). The main steps in the calculation are outlined in appendix 5.4 and we find that to a first approximation the radius vector r satisfies the differential equation

$$\dot{r} = \epsilon p r (1 - \frac{\epsilon \rho a}{4\omega} r^2) . \tag{5.24}$$

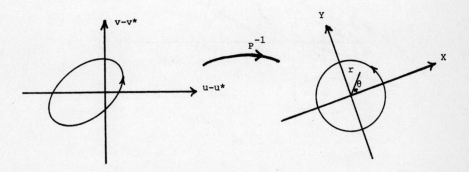

Figure 5.3   The coordinate transformations

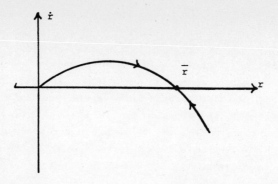

<u>Figure 5.4</u> Motion of the radius of the limit cycle

The differential equation (5.24) contains all the qualitative features of dynamic motion on the centre manifold and is most conveniently analysed by plotting $\dot{r}$ as a function of r, as shown in figure 5.4. There we see that the point $r = \bar{r}$ is asymptotically stable, this being in fact the radius of the stable limit cycle in the X-Y plane. On transforming back to the (u, v) plane the limit cycle shows up as a rotated ellipse about (u^*, v^*). The relationship of the limit cycle in the two-dimensional (u,v) plane to the one in three-dimensional (x,u,v) space is shown in figure 5.5. The limit cycle we have found is a projection onto the (u,v) plane of the actual limit cycle on the centre-manifold x = h(u,v). For complteness we show how the saddle point equilibrium at the origin relates to the limit cycle.

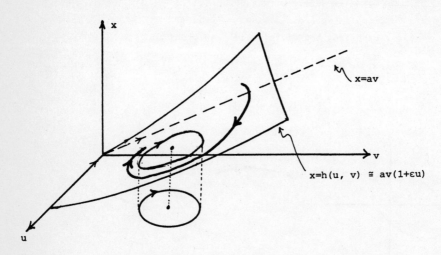

<u>Figure 5.5</u> The phase portrait of the Goodwin model

From equation (5.24) we see that the amplitude of the stable limit cycle is given by

$$\bar{r} = \left[\frac{4\omega}{\epsilon \rho a} \right]^{1/2} .$$ (5.25)

and to the same order of approximation the period of the cycle is

$$\tau = 2\pi/\omega .$$ (5.26)

When the limit cycle motion is related back to the employment rate v and wage share u, the amplitude of the cycle of each of these, which we denote v_a, u_a respectively turn out to be given by (see appendix 5.5)

$$v_a^2 = \frac{4}{\epsilon p a} \left[(\epsilon p)^2 + (\frac{v^*}{\sigma})^2 \right],$$ (5.27)

and

$$u_a^2 = \frac{4\omega}{\epsilon \rho a} = 2 \frac{u^* v^*}{\epsilon} \left[\frac{4(1 + \epsilon u^*)^2}{\sigma^2 p^2} - \epsilon^2 \right]^{1/2} .$$ (5.28)

Since to first order $\epsilon \approx T$, it is clear from (5.27-28) that as T increases, the amplitudes of both the employment and wage share cycles decrease. So a longer delay in the adjustment of wages to changing employment conditions leads to less violent fluctuations in economic activity. On the other hand, to first order T has no effect on the period of the oscillation (see appendix 5.6).

The effects on the cycle of an increase in workers wage bargaining power can be measured by increasing ρ. The signs of the relevant partial derivatives are are calculated in appendix 5.7 and turn out to be

$$\frac{\partial v^*}{\partial \rho} < 0, \quad \frac{\partial u^*}{\partial \rho} = 0, \quad \frac{\partial v_a}{\partial \rho} < 0 \quad \text{and} \quad \frac{\partial u_a}{\partial \rho} < 0 .$$ (5.29)

So that an increase in workers' bargaining power leads to a reduction in the equilibrium employment level v^*, no change in the equilibrium wage share u^*, whilst the amplitude of fluctuations around these is reduced. The effect of other parametric changes on the amplitude of the fluctuations such as α, the growth rate of labour productivity, and σ, the capital-output ratio, is not clear cut.

5.5 Discussion

We have introduced a time lag into the wage formation equation of the Goodwin model and by use of centre-manifold theory have shown that the resulting system of three differential equations displays stable limit cycle behaviour, at least for a relatively small time lag. The dynamic behaviour of the model for larger values of the time lag remains an open question. However given the work of Oster (1978) which indicates the appearance of chaotic behaviour in predator-prey equations with time lags, it seems highly likely that in our modified Goodwin model the stable regular limit cycle could also give way to chaotic behaviour once the time lag increases past some critical value. The way to investigate this issue would be to undertake a study using a combination of analytical techniques and numerical simulations as Sparrow (1983) has done for the Lorenz equations.

Our mode of analysis now leaves the way open for the removal of some of the undesirable assumptions of the Goodwin model such as exogenous population growth, exogenous technical progress and constant capital-output ratio. Van der Ploeg (1983) has already noted that when the capital-output ratio, σ, is a decreasing function of v, then the equilibrium is locally unstable which would certainly indicate limit cycle behaviour. One way to analyse such behaviour would be to make reasonable assumptions about $\sigma(v)$.

Appendix 5.1

The real roots of the cubic

$$T \lambda^3 + \lambda^2 + \Omega^2 = 0, \tag{5A1}$$

occur at the intersection of the cubic $y = -T\lambda^3$ and the parabola $y = \lambda^2 + \Omega^2$. It is thereby easy to see that there is one negative real root for $T > 0$, which $\rightarrow -\infty$ as $T \rightarrow 0$.

To obtain information about the complex roots, note first that by implicit differentiation of (5A1) we have

$$\frac{\partial \lambda}{\partial T} = -\frac{\lambda^2}{2 + 3T\lambda} . \tag{5A2}$$

We may use (5A2) to determine how the nature of the complex roots change as T passes through 0. Noting that at $T = 0$ the complex roots are given by $\lambda = \pm i\Omega$ we calculate from (5A2) that at $T = 0$,

$$\frac{\partial \lambda}{\partial T} = -\frac{\lambda^2}{2} = \frac{\Omega^2}{2} > 0.$$

If we let $R(T)$ denote the real part of the complex roots as a function of T, then we have shown that

$$R(0) = 0, \quad R'(0) > 0 .$$

These facts indicate that $R(T) > 0$ for $T > 0$ and in some neighbourhood of $T = 0$.

After some tedious algebraic manipulations it is possible to show that $R(T)$ satisfies the cubic

$$g(R) = 8TR^3 + 8R^2 + 2R/T - \Omega^2 = 0.$$

The facts that $g(0) = -\Omega^2 < 0$, $g'(R) = 0$ at $R = -T/2$ and $-T/6$ and that $g(-T/2) = -\Omega^2 < 0$, demonstrate that $R(T) > 0$ for all $T > 0$.

Appendix 5.2

The equation of the centre manifold is, from (5.11),

$$x = h(u, v) \ .$$

Differentiating both sides with respect to time we have that

$$\dot{x} = h_u \ \dot{u} + h_v \ \dot{v}. \tag{5A3}$$

Substituting from equation (5.4) for $\dot{x}$ on the left-hand side of (5A3) and from equations (5.8) and (5.9) for $\dot{v}$ and $\dot{u}$ on the right-hand side, we obtain the following equation for u and v :-

$$\frac{1}{T} (v - h(u,v)) = \rho(-v^* + h(u,v))u \ h_u + \frac{1}{\sigma} (u^* - u)v h_v. \tag{5A4}$$

We now seek an approximation to h(u, v) in the form

$$h(u,v) = h_0 + (h_1 u + h_2 v) + (h_{11} u^2/2 + h_{12} uv + h_{22} v^2/2) + \ldots \tag{5A5}$$

By substituting (5A5) into (5A4) and equating like powers of u and v on both sides, we obtain up to quadratic order the approximation to the centre-manifold given in equation (5.12).

Appendix 5.3

Define the matrix P^{-1} according to

$$P^{-1} = \begin{bmatrix} 0 & 1 \\ -\sigma\omega/\bar{v} & -\epsilon\sigma p/\bar{v} \end{bmatrix} \ . \tag{5A6}$$

where the first and second columns are respectively the complex and real parts of the eigenvectors of J.

In terms of the variables $U = u - u^*$, $V = v - v^*$, the differential system (5.14) can be written

$$\dot{V} = - vU/\sigma \quad - UV/\sigma,$$

$$\dot{U} = \rho a u^* (1 + \epsilon u^*) V + \epsilon \rho u^* v^* a \, U + \epsilon \rho a (2u^* U V + v^* U^2 + U^2 V) \ . \tag{5A7}$$

The change of coordinates

$$\begin{bmatrix} X \\ Y \end{bmatrix} = P^{-1} \begin{bmatrix} v - v^* \\ u - u^* \end{bmatrix} \tag{5A8}$$

reduces the differential system (5A7) to (5.19) of the main text where

$$f_1(X, Y) = \epsilon \rho a \, \frac{-2\epsilon^2 \rho p a u^*}{\omega} X^2 - \frac{2u^* v^*}{\sigma \, \omega} XY + v^* Y^2 - \frac{\epsilon p}{\omega} X^3 - \frac{v^*}{\sigma \omega} X^2 Y \ ,$$

and

$$f_2(X, Y) = - \frac{(\omega - 2\epsilon^2 \sigma \rho p a u^*)}{v^* \omega} X(\epsilon p X + \frac{v^*}{\sigma} Y) - \epsilon^2 \sigma \rho p a \, X^2$$

$$+ \frac{\epsilon^2 \sigma \rho p a}{v^* \omega} X^2 \, (\epsilon p \, X + \frac{v^*}{\sigma} Y) \ .$$

Appendix 5.4

Straightforward application of the methods of section 2.5 yields that to first order r and θ satisfy the differential equations

$$\dot{\theta} = \omega \ ,$$

and

$$\dot{r} = \epsilon p r + h(r), \tag{5A9}$$

where

$$h(r) = \frac{1}{2\pi} \int_0^{2\pi} \left[f_1(r \cos\theta, \, r \sin\theta) \cos\theta + f_2(r \cos\theta, \, r \sin\theta) \sin\theta \right] d\theta.$$

Viewing the expressions for f_1 and f_2 the calculation of $h(r)$ seems extremely tedious, however the calculations greatly simplify when it is noted that due to the orthogonality of trigonometric functions only the X^3 and $X^2 Y$ terms make a contribution to $h(r)$. It turns out that

$$h(r) = \frac{r^3}{2\pi} \int_0^{2\pi} \left[- \frac{\epsilon^2 \rho p a}{\omega} \cos^4\theta + \frac{\epsilon^2 \rho p a}{\omega} \cos^2\theta \, \sin^2\theta \right] d\theta = \frac{-\epsilon^2 \rho p a}{4\omega} r^3.$$

Using this expression, (5A9) reduces to the differential equation (5.20) of the main text.

Appendix 5.5

From equation (5A8)

$$\begin{bmatrix} v - v^* \\ u - u^* \end{bmatrix} - P \begin{bmatrix} X \\ Y \end{bmatrix} = \frac{v^*}{\sigma\omega} \begin{bmatrix} -\epsilon\sigma p/v^* & -1 \\ \sigma\omega/v^* & 0 \end{bmatrix} \begin{bmatrix} X \\ Y \end{bmatrix} .$$

After some simple algebra we find that

$$v - v^* = - rB \cos(\theta - \psi) \text{ and } u - u^* = r \sin \theta,$$

where

$$B^2 = \frac{\epsilon p}{\omega}^2 + \frac{v^*}{\sigma\omega}^2 \text{ and } \cos\psi = \epsilon p/wB.$$

It is clear from those expressions that the amplitude of the u oscillation is r and that of the v oscillation is rB.

Appendix 5.6

The relevant partial derivatives are

$$\frac{\partial \epsilon}{\partial T} = \sigma\epsilon^2/T^2, \quad \frac{\partial a}{\partial T} = -u^* a^2/\sigma, \quad \frac{\partial p}{\partial T} = - pau^*/\sigma ,$$

so that

$$\eta \frac{\partial \nu}{\partial T} = au^*(1 + \epsilon u^*)/p\sigma^2 + u^* \epsilon^2/pT^2 .$$

It then follows that

$$\omega\frac{\partial\omega}{\partial T} = p \frac{\partial p}{\partial T} (\eta^2 - \epsilon^2) + p^2(\eta\frac{\partial\eta}{\partial T} - \epsilon \frac{\partial\epsilon}{\partial T})$$

$$- \frac{-2pau^*}{\sigma^2}(1 + \epsilon u^*) + \frac{2u^*p\epsilon^2}{T^2} + \frac{2p^2au^*\epsilon^2}{\sigma} - \frac{2\sigma p^2}{T^2}\epsilon^3 = 0 \text{ to } O(T).$$

Appendix 5.7

The relevant partial derivatives are

$$\frac{\partial u^*}{\partial \rho} = 0, \quad \frac{\partial v^*}{\partial \rho} = -\frac{v^*}{\rho}, \quad \frac{\partial v_a}{\partial \rho} = \frac{4v^2}{\epsilon pa\sigma^2 \rho v_a}$$

and

$$\frac{\partial u_a}{\partial \rho} = -\frac{2\omega}{u_a \epsilon a\rho^2}.$$

CHAPTER 6 **THE COBWEB MODEL; ITS INSTABILITY AND THE ONSET OF CHAOS**

6.1 Introduction

In chapters three, four and five we have seen various examples of limit cycle motion
in dynamic economic models. However as we pointed out in section 2.7 limit cycles are
not the only type of oscillatory motion which can arise in dynamical systems. For
differential equation models of dimension three or greater chaotic motion is possible
and indeed is more likely to be the norm. In the last chapter we speculated that as
the time lag increases the limit cycle motion of the Goodwin model would evolve into
chaotic motion, probably via the process of period doubling.

An understanding of the dynamics of three dimensional differential equation systems,
such as the Goodwin model of the last chapter or three dimensional extensions of the
models in chapters three and four, as parameter changes move them into chaotic
regions would require a careful blend of analytical and numerical techniques. Such a
study for any of the models just mentionned would constitute a monograph in its own
right, as can be evidenced from Sparrow's (1983) book on the "innocent looking"
Lorenz equations.

Our aim in this chapter is far more modest and that is to illustrate the emergence of
chaotic motion in a simple dynamic economic model. A most convenient model for this
purpose is the cobweb model. In order to avoid the technical difficulties of working
with a three-dimensional differential equation system, we use a difference equation
formulation, since it is possible to obtain chaotic motion from a one-dimensional
difference equation.

The cobweb model of price dynamics in a single (typically agricultural) market has
spawned a vast literature and has recently again become topical in the rational
expectations literature; Sheffrin (1983). Of particular interest are the stability
conditions of the model which were first discussed by Leontieff (1933) and then by
Ezekiel (1938) and more thoroughly investigated by Nerlove (1958). Further
refinements were added by Carlson (1968) and Manning (1970, 1971).

An important condition for stability of the cobweb model is that the supply
elasticity be less than the demand elasticity. However as Sheffrin points out it is
more likely that this condition will be violated. Our aim in this chapter is to
investigate the fate of cobweb cycles when the equilibrium is unstable. To our
knowledge scant attention has been paid in the literature to the behaviour of the

model as prices move away from the equilibrium. There are, however, two important exceptions. In a largely ignored paper Leontief (1934) demonstrated the possibility of two-cycles when the equilibrium of the cobweb is locally unstable. As we shall see below, the emergence of two-cycles is the first step on the path to chaos. Recently Jensen and Urban (1984) showed the existence of chaotic behaviour in a cobweb model having a particular structure. This lack of attention seems strange on two counts. Firstly, realism dictates that prices cannot grow without bound so ultimately we might expect prices to move to some other equilibrium point or settle down into either some regular or irregular oscillatory motion. Secondly, recent years have seen a dramatic increase in the understanding of the qualitative behaviour of dynamical systems displaying various instabilities, typically such systems are simple but nonlinear and involve time lags; see e.g. May (1976a).

We shall introduce a fairly simple and obvious nonlinearity into the supply function of the cobweb model and analyse the dynamics of the model when the equilibrium is unstable. We shall assume, in conventional manner, that suppliers form prices adaptively but we shall allow for the expectations time lag and production time lag to differ. We find that the price time paths exhibit either regular or irregular oscillatory motion.

6.2 The Nonlinear Cobweb Model

We shall use p_t and π_t to denote price and expected price respectively, both at time t. We assume a traditional linear demand function for the good given by

$$q^d_t = a + bp_t , \qquad (a > 0, \ b < 0). \tag{6.1}$$

However we shall assume a nonlinear supply function, dependent upon the expected price, which we write as

$$q^s_t = f(\pi_t) , \tag{6.2}$$

and suppose that the function f has the general shape shown in figure 6.1.

The supply function in figure 6.1 has the following characteristics; (a) for expected price less than $\tilde{\pi}$ a minimum amount $\bar{q}$ will be supplied. This characteristic could be derived from production theory, (b) the supply function increases monotonically from $\tilde{\pi}$ but in such a way that its slope tends to zero as $\pi \to \infty$. This characteristic reflecting diminishing returns in the underlying production process.

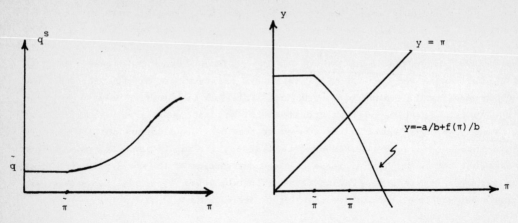

Figure 6.1 Nonlinear supply function Figure 6.2 Determination of the equilibrium, $\bar{\pi}$

We have drawn the supply function to appear smooth at $\pi = \tilde{\pi}$ since our later technical arguments require the assumption that $f'(\tilde{\pi})$ is continuous. It is possible, at the expense of increased mathematical complexity, to analyze the case when $f'(\tilde{\pi})$ is discontinuous across $\pi = \tilde{\pi}$, however the qualitative dynamic behaviour of the model turns out to be no different from what we describe below.

The dynamics of the cobweb model are usually discussed in a discrete time framework and we shall ultimately do the same. However, it turns out to be convenient to initially formulate the model in continuous time.

We assume that price expectations are formed with a distributed lag whose mean lag time is θ, i.e.

$$\pi_t = \int_{-\infty}^{t} \frac{e^{-(t-s)/\theta}}{\theta} \cdot p_s \, ds , \qquad (6.3)$$

from which may be derived the usual adaptive expectation equation

$$\dot{\pi}_t = \frac{1}{\theta} (p_t - \pi_t) . \qquad (6.4)$$

Equality of supply and demand in the market for the good leads to

$$a + bp_t = f(\pi_t) . \qquad (6.5)$$

Equations (6.4) and (6.5) simultaneously determine p_t and π_t. Using (6.5) to eliminate p_t in (6.4) we find that π_t satisfies the differential equation

$$\dot{\pi}_t = -\frac{a}{\theta b} - \frac{\pi_t}{\theta} + \frac{1}{\theta b} f(\pi_t) \quad , \tag{6.6}$$

which determines the dynamics of the model.

The equilibrium, $\bar{\pi}$, is determined by the condition $\dot{\pi}_t = 0$, i.e. $\bar{\pi}$ is the solution of

$$\pi = -\frac{a}{b} + \frac{1}{b} f(\pi). \tag{6.7}$$

The geometrical determination of $\bar{\pi}$ is illustrated in Figure 6.2. From equation (6.4) the equilibrium price $\bar{p}$ is given by $\bar{p} = \bar{\pi}$.

Since

$$\frac{\partial \dot{\pi}_t}{\partial \pi_t} \bigg|_{\pi_t = \bar{\pi}} = -\frac{1}{\theta} (1 - \frac{1}{b} f'(\bar{\pi})) < 0 \quad , \tag{6.8}$$

the equilibrium is *locally stable*. It is a simple matter to derive the sketch of $\dot{\pi}_t$ as a function of π_t shown in Figure 6.3, from which it is clear that the equilibrium is also *globally stable*. Thus far we have established the well known result that the continuous time version of the cobweb model is stable irrespective of the relative slopes of the supply and demand curves and of the expectation time lag θ. The dynamics of the cobweb model become more interesting when we consider the discrete time version, which we do in the next section.

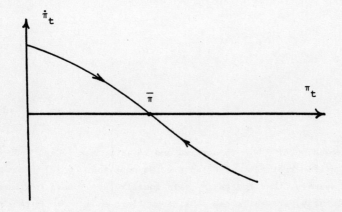

Figure 6.3 Global stability of $\bar{\pi}$ in continuous time

6.3 Discrete Time Dynamics

We shall discretise the differential equation (6) by replacing $\dot{\pi}_t$ with $(\pi_{t+h} - \pi_t)/h$. Here h is the time step and economically may be thought of as the time between market transactions (or alternatively as the production lag). We shall henceforth refer to h as the transactions lag.

The relationship between the expectations lag, θ, and the transactions lag, h, turns out to be an important factor in our subsequent analysis. It should be pointed out that in our framework $\theta < h$ would make no sense since producers would not form price expectations over a shorter time period than that between transactions. Hence we shall only consider $\theta/h \geq 1$.

The discretized form of the differential equation (6.6) thus becomes

$$\pi_{t+h} = g(\pi_t) \; , \tag{6.9}$$

where

$$g(\pi) = -\frac{ah}{b\theta} + (1 - \frac{h}{\theta})\rho + \frac{h}{b\theta} f(\pi) \; . \tag{6.10}$$

The equilibrium of this system is still $\bar{\pi}$ as given by equation 6.7.

A study of the dynamics of equation (6.9) proceeds from a study of the *local* stability properties of the equilibrium $\bar{\pi}$. In fact $\bar{\pi}$ is locally stable for parameter values such that

$$|g'(\bar{\pi})| < 1, \tag{6.11}$$

which reduces to

$$1 - 2\frac{\theta}{h} < \frac{f'(\bar{\pi})}{b} < 1 \; . \tag{6.12}$$

In the conventional cobweb model $\theta = h$ is assumed and in this case (6.12) reduces to the usual stability condition that $-1 < -f'(\bar{\pi})/b < 1$. We note that (6.12) summarises some familiar results, namely, that for any θ, $\bar{\pi}$ is locally (and indeed by virtue of the previous section globally) stable in the continuous limit as $h \to 0$. Furthermore for a fixed h, increasing the expectations lag θ increases the region of local stability.

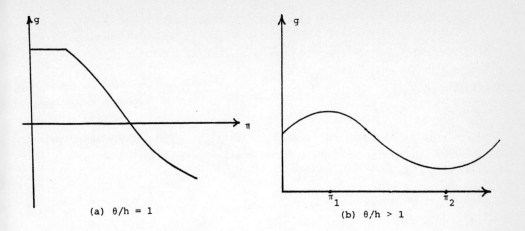

(a) $\theta/h = 1$ (b) $\theta/h > 1$

Figure 6.4 The function g

However it is the behaviour of the model in the region of instability which is our
main concern here. This aspect is best approached by first considering the evolution
of the difference equation (6.9) from a geometric point of view. To do this we need a
sketch of the general features of the function g. Such a sketch is easily obtained by
considering the derivative $g'(\pi)$ and is given in figure 6.4, where we see that two
cases need to be considered (a) $\theta/h = 1$, and (b) $\theta/h > 1$. The turning points π_1, π_2
in the case $\theta/h > 1$ are the solutions of

$$f'(\pi) = -b(\frac{\theta}{h} - 1),$$ (6.13)

which is illustrated in figure 6.5.

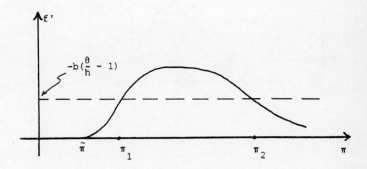

Figure 6.5 The function f'

The dynamics of the difference equation 6.9 is seen geometrically by placing a 45° line on the graphs of figure 6.4 and constructing the usual cobweb motions. However before taking this step it is instructive to analyze the model in the case $\theta/h = 1$, which is the traditional case. In this case,

$$\pi_{t+h} = p_t \tag{6.14}$$

so we are able to obtain a difference equation for p_t directly without having to resort to the function g. By equating supply and demand we find that p_t satisfies the difference equation

$$a + bp_t = f(p_{t-h}). \tag{6.15}$$

In figure 6.6 we construct the cobweb in the case of instability.

There we see that prices diverge from the equilibrium $\bar{p}$ to ultimately settle down into the *two-cycle* $\{p_L, p_u, p_L, p_u, \dots\}$, with quantities settling down into the corresponding two-cycle $\{q_L, q_u, q_L, q_u, \dots\}$. The basic determinant of this cycle is the lower supply constraint q_L, from which p_u, q_u and p_L are determined via

$$q^d(p_u) = q_L, \quad q_u = q^s(p_u), \quad q^d(p_L) = q_u. \tag{6.16}$$

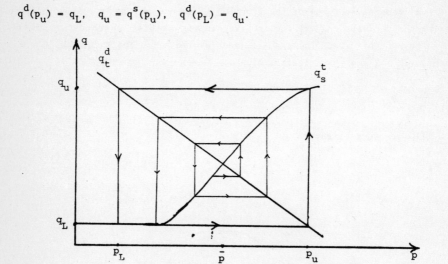

Figure 6.6   The two-cycle when $\theta = h$

Manning (1970) has already noted that the condition $q^s(p_u) = q^d(p_L)$ implies a two-cycle. As we shall see a more diverse dynamic behaviour emerges when $\theta > h$ is considered.

6.4 Period Doubling to Chaos

The dynamics of the difference equation (6.9) in the case of local instability of the equilibrium point are illustrated in figure 6.7. Consider first of all figure 6.7(a), which is the story of figure 6.6 viewed from the viewpoint of expected prices π_t rather than actual prices p_t, with π_u and π_L corresponding to p_u and p_L respectively.

Notice that if we define the iterated mapping

$$g^{(2)}(\pi) = g(g(\pi)),\tag{6.17}$$

then π_u and π_L are both stable fixed points of $g^{(2)}(\pi)$, i.e. are both solutions of

$$\pi = g^{(2)}(\pi),\tag{6.18}$$

since $\pi_u = g(\pi_L)$ and $\pi_L = g(\pi_u)$.

Now consider figure 6.7(b) when $\theta/h > 1$. For θ/h still close to 1 we might expect that as π_t diverges away from $\bar{\pi}$ it might settle down into a two cycle as in the case $\theta/h = 1$. This will be so if π_u and π_L are stable fixed points of the iterated

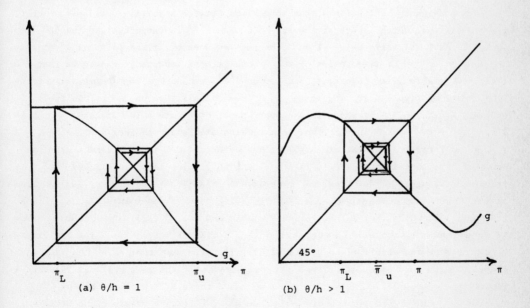

(a) $\theta/h = 1$ (b) $\theta/h > 1$

Figure 6.7 The two-cycle

mapping $g^{(2)}(\pi)$ (now with $\theta/h > 1$, whereas in (6.17) we had $\theta/h = 1$). It indeed turns out that such π_u and π_L exist, however rather than attempting to derive the sketch of $g^{(2)}(\pi)$ which would be a rather messy procedure we are able to appeal to some powerful results given by Feigenbaum (1983). This latter author discusses at length the difference equation

$$X_{t+1} = \lambda X_t (1 - X_t) = G(X_t) .$$ (6.19)

The function G on the right hand side is a concave parabola cutting the horizontal axis at $X = 0$ and $X = 1$ as shown in figure 6.8. Whilst the form of the function G may seem very particular Feigenbaum shows that any difference equation whose right hand side has the basic concave, folding over, nature of G will rapidly settle down to behave qualitatively in the same manner as equation (6.19). Hence we shall first discuss the qualitative behaviour of (6.19) and then relate the behaviour of the difference equation (6.9) to it.

Figure 6.8 displays the situation when the equilibrium $\bar{X}$ is locally stable. In the lower panel we sketch the function $G^{(2)}(X) = G(G(X))$, of which $\bar{X}$ is also a fixed point, stable in the case depicted. In fact any fixed point of G is a fixed point of $G^{(2)}$, but $G^{(2)}$ may have fixed points which are not fixed points of G. It is this latter fact which is the basic reason for the emergence of bounded oscillatory behaviour when $\bar{X}$ becomes unstable.

Figure 6.9 shows the situation at the borderline between stability and instability, i.e., $G'(\bar{X}) = -1$ which occurs at $\lambda = \Lambda_1 = 3.0$. Now $G^{(2)}$ is tangential to the 45° line at $X = \bar{X}$. As $G'(\bar{X})$ falls below -1 and $\bar{X}$ becomes an unstable fixed point of G, it also becomes an unstable fixed point of $G^{(2)}$. What is more important however is that two additional *stable* fixed points, X_1 and X_2, of $G^{(2)}$ now emerge, as displayed in the lower panel of figure 6.10. The motion of X_t now spirals towards the stable two-cycle $\{X_1, X_2, X_1, X_2, \ldots \}$ as shown in the upper panel of figure 6.10. It turns out that $G^{(2)'}(X_2) = G^{(2)'}(X_1)$ and the two-cycle remains stable for as long as $|G^{(2)'}(X_2)| < 1$, i.e. as long as X_1 and X_2 are stable fixed points of $G^{(2)}$. So the next critical value of λ is that for which $G^{(2)'}(X_2) = -1$ and that value is $\lambda = \Lambda_2 = 3.449$. As λ increases through Λ_2, the iterated function $G^{(4)}(X) = G^{(2)}(G^{(2)}(X))$ passes from having three fixed points $(X_1, \bar{X}, X_2)$ to having seven fixed points $(X_1^-, X_1, X_1^+, \bar{X}, X_2^-, X_2, X_2^+)$ of which $(X_1^-, X_1^+, X_2^-, X_2^+)$ are stable and $(X_1, \bar{X}, X_2)$ are unstable. Now X_t tends towards the stable four-cycle $\{X_1^-, X_1^+, X_2^-, X_2^+, X_1^-, X_1^+, \ldots\}$. See Figure 6.11. As with the stable fixed points of $G^{(2)}$ it turns out that $G^{(4)}$ has the same slope at each of its stable fixed points. Obviously the next critical value of λ occurs at $\lambda = \Lambda_3 = 3.544$ where $G^{(4)'}(X_1^-) = -1$ and it is by now clear that by considering the fixed points of $G^{(8)}(X) = G^{(4)}(G^{(4)}(X))$ a stable eight cycle will appear. This process whereby the stable cycle doubles its period as λ passes through the critical values Λ_1, Λ_2, Λ_3, $\ldots$ is known as *period doubling*. The mathematical

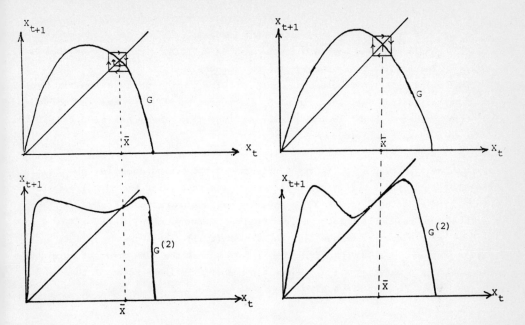

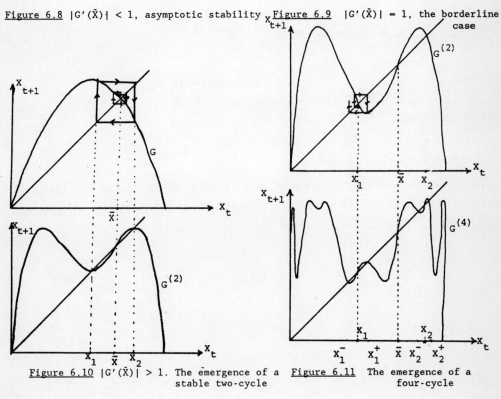

<u>Figure 6.8</u> $|G'(\bar{X})| < 1$, asymptotic stability   <u>Figure 6.9</u> $|G'(\check{X})| = 1$, the borderline case

<u>Figure 6.10</u> $|G'(\bar{X})| > 1$. The emergence of a   <u>Figure 6.11</u>   The emergence of a
stable two-cycle   four-cycle

details of determining the sequence $\{\Lambda_n\}$ are discussed by Feigenbaum and it is worth noting that it is possible by a sequence of transformations to reduce the problem to continually considering the non zero fixed point of $X = G(X)$ with G appropriately redefined.   The important observation for our discussion is that $\Lambda_n \rightarrow \Lambda_\infty = 3.570$. Beyond this value of λ the stable cycle has infinite period which means the cycle never repeats itself.   The time path of X_t is bounded oscillatory, does not converge to any fixed value of X and is not periodic;   the term *chaos* has been coined to describe such dynamic behaviour.

Feigenbaum shows an even more important property of the period doubling phenomenon, namely that such behaviour is not dependent on the particular functional form of G. Any difference equation $X_{t+1} = G(X_t)$, where G has a quadratic extremum (and also satisfies the so-called Schwarzian derivative condition) will, after a few iterations, settle down to behave like the system (6.19). The sequence $\{\Lambda_n\}$ is different for each particular functional form but of the same order of magnitude. Furthermore $\Lambda_n \rightarrow \Lambda_\infty$ at the rate δ^{-n} where the number δ is independent of the particular form.   In fact $\delta \approx 4.67$.

6.5 Onset of Chaos in the Cobweb Model

The upshot of the discussion in the previous section is that the difference equation (6.9) will quickly settle down to exhibit the same qualitative behaviour as the difference equation

$$\pi_{t+h} = G(\pi_t) \tag{6.20}$$

where G is the quadratic approximation to g which passes through the origin, the point $(\bar{\pi}, g(\bar{\pi}))$ and satisfies $G'(\bar{\pi}) = g'(\bar{\pi})$. The function G satisfying these requirements is given by

$$G(\pi) = \pi(\alpha - \beta\pi) \tag{6.21}$$

where

$$\alpha = 2 - g'(\bar{\pi}) > 0 \text{ and } \beta = (1 - g'(\bar{\pi}))/\bar{\pi} > 0. \tag{6.22}$$

If we define the rescaled variable $X_t = \beta\pi_t/\alpha$, then (6.20) reduces to the difference equation

$$X_{t+h} = \alpha \, X_t (1 - X_t). \tag{6.23}$$

If we redefine the time unit so that h=1 then we have precisely the difference equation (6.19), for which we know that chaotic behaviour sets in for $\alpha \geq 3.57$, i.e. for $g'(\bar{\pi}) \leq -1.57$. We are now able to give a complete characterization of the dynamics of the cobweb model:-

$1 - \dfrac{2\theta}{h} < f'(\bar{\pi})/b < 1$, asymptotically stable to $\bar{\pi}$,

$1 - 2.57\theta/h < f'(\bar{\pi})/b \leq 1 - 2\theta/h$, period doubling around $\bar{\pi}$, (6.24)

$f'(\bar{\pi})/b \leq 1 - 2.57\theta/h$, chaotic motion around $\bar{\pi}$.

These various regions are succinctly represented in figure 6.12. These conditions may also be expressed in terms of elasticities if we bear in mind that $f'(\bar{\pi})/b$ equals the ratio of supply elasticity to demand elasticity.

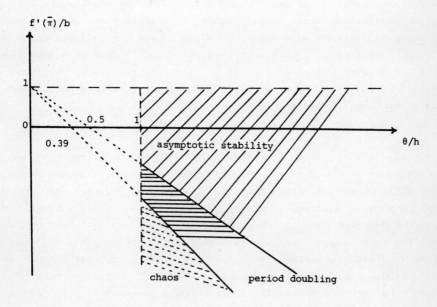

Figure 6.12 Dynamic regimes of the cobweb model

6.6 **Discussion**

Our analysis has shown that the introduction of plausible nonlinearities into the basic cobweb model leads to the emergence of chaotic motion in the locally unstable region via the period doubling route. Meadows (1970) pointed to the need to introduce nonlinearities and time lags into the cobweb model so as to obtain more realistic price time paths and he did so by use of computer simulation. Here we have made the same point with a very simple model. We have considered a nonlinear supply function with a horizontal section at low prices to indicate that producers will not let production drop below a minimum level in order to cover fixed costs. If we consider only $\theta > h$ then it is possible to dispense with this horizontal section and obtain the same results by just considering a general S-shaped supply function. Other cases which would warrant further investigation are backward bending supply curves and nonlinear demand curves.

The existence of chaotic motion has already been observed in a number of dynamic economic models. Day (1982) shows its existence in a discrete time version of Solow's descriptive growth model whilst Benhabib and Day (1982) find such behaviour in an overlapping generations model. These authors have established the existence of chaotic motion by making use of a theorem proved by Li and Yorke (1975), which gives a sufficient condition for one-dimensional difference equations to have chaotic solutions. We have preferred to proceed by use of Feigenbaum's result on the universality of quadratic maps as this enables us to gain more insight into the structure of the stability regions of the model.

We believe that the existence of chaotic motion in many basic models of economic dynamics could have profound consequences for some branches of economic theory. Sheffrin (1983) makes the point that empirical evidence suggests that the cobweb model with adaptive expectations is more likely to be in the locally unstable region. He then argues that such local instability favours the use of a rational expectations framework for such models. Our analysis shows that the adaptive expectations framework can yield realistic behaviour in the locally unstable region. In the chaotic regime the price time path appears to be stochastic to the observer. It may be that on other grounds the rational expectations framework is preferable to the adaptive expectations one, but the local instability of adaptive expectations alone does not provide such grounds.

Rational expectationists argue against the use of adaptive expectations on the grounds that rational agents could estimate the model and be able to predict subsequent time paths. These time paths would include intervals where the rational agents are making wrong predictions, and, it is argued, rational agents with a knowledge of the model would not behave in this way. This argument seems less convincing once it is established that models based on adaptive expectations can yield chaotic, unpredictable behaviour. There is starting to emerge a literature (see Schuster (1984)) on empirical verification of the period doubling route to chaos. It would be interesting to examine in this light the models of agricultural supply discussed by Sheffrin which seem to lend support to the rational expectations hypothesis.

CHAPTER 7 __PERFECT FORESIGHT MODELS AND THE DYNAMIC INSTABILITY PROBLEM FROM A HIGHER__
__VIEWPOINT__

7.1 Introduction

In this chapter we bring to bear a number of the concepts and techniques used in
earlier chapters on an important problem in the modern theory of economic dynamics.
This is the so called dynamic instability problem.

It is a well established result that models of perfect foresight in which economic
agents correctly perceive the rate of change of an economic variable (e.g. the rate
of inflation in models of monetary dynamics or the exchange rate in models of
exchange rate dynamics) display a dynamic instability of the saddle-point type. So
that unless the initial values happen to place the system on the stable arm of the
saddle-point, the economic variables of interest will diverge more and more from the
equilibrium. This type of behaviour was first observed in capital theory models by
Hahn (1960, 1966) and Samuelson (1967), but in recent years has become of particular
relevance in the rational expectations literature; see e.g. Sargent and Wallace
(1973), Black (1974), Brock (1975), Calvo (1977), Taylor (1977), Shiller (1978),
Blanchard (1979), Gray and Turnovsky (1979), Burmeister (1980a, b), McCallum (1983)
and Scarth (1985).

This type of dynamic behaviour can be seen in its most essential form in a basic
monetary dynamics model with a non-durable good and money as the only asset by which
wealth may be transferred through time. For this model the saddle point becomes
degenerate in that the stable arm collapses into a point, see e.g. Black (1974) and
Burmeister (1980a). In this case one finds that in the phase plane of price and
expected rate of change of price, convergence to the equilibrium point is only
assured from a restricted set of initial conditions. All other initial conditions
result in divergent price paths. Sargent and Wallace sidestep the dynamic instability
problem by assuming that, (i) the price level can change discontinuously, and (ii)
economic agents expect a process of continually accelerating or decelerating
inflation to eventually come to an end; in this way the dynamic variables are assumed
to make an initial jump onto a path converging to the equilibrium of the model. Gray
and Turnovsky adopt a similar procedure in their discussion of exchange rate
dynamics. Some authors have found this way of sidestepping the dynamic instability
problem as unsatisfactory; see e.g. Evans and Yarrow (1981), other authors seek to
justify the Sargent and Wallace procedure by using an encompassing framework
involving dynamic optimizing behaviour; see e.g. Brock (1975) and Obstfeld and Rogoff

(1983). The procedure of arbitrarily jumping onto a convergent path continues to pose somewhat of a conundrum as it is generally not possible to find any satisfactory economic justification for such jumps. In applying this procedure to a dynamic model of output and the stock market Blanchard (1981) describes it as a standard if not entirely convincing practice.

In this chapter we shall discuss the dynamic instability problem in the framework of the basic model of monetary dynamics. However, lest the reader gain the impression that the dynamic instability problem is confined to models of monetary dynamics we draw his attention to the remarks of Burmeister (1980a) who points out that the dynamic instability problem in principle arises in all dynamic macroeconomic models if capital gains and losses on assets are properly accounted for. The fact that the problem has not received wider recognition in the macroeconomics literature is due to the fact that capital gains are either ignored or treated naively by the use of static expectations. Thus the considerable attention devoted to the extremely simple model of monetary dynamics is warranted as we thereby gain an understanding of the qualitative dynamic behaviour of a wide range of dynamic macroeconomic models.

We shall consider the simple model of monetary dynamics from what we believe is a new point of view. We motivate a nonlinear money demand function dependent upon the expected rate of inflation, allow the money market to adjust sluggishly and assume inflationary expectations are formed with a time lag (i.e. adaptive expectations). We show that for a sufficiently short expectations time lag the equilibrium of the model is locally unstable with all price time paths diverging from the equilibrium. However, the diverging price paths do not tend to infinity but rather to a unique periodic price path. In other words the model has a unique, stable limit cycle if the expectations time lag is sufficiently small. To examine the perfect foresight case we consider the limit as the expectations time lag tends to zero and show that there is a limiting stable limit cycle to which all perfect foresight paths are tending irrespective of initial conditions. In the framework which we present here the dynamic instability problem is no longer seen as a problem as we are able to view the dynamics of the perfect foresight model from a dimension one higher than that in which it is normally viewed. We are able to achieve this higher dimensional viewpoint by introducing a nonlinear model and analysing the perfect foresight model as the limiting case of the adaptive expectations model.

Our solution to the dynamic instability problem is obtained by introducing as an economic equilibrium concept a stable limit cycle, on which economic quantities are varying periodically. This picture seems to pose a further conundrum; economic agents observe their expectations and the variable on which they form expectations to vary periodically, and therefore predictably, but do nothing to eliminate the resulting systematic error in their forecasts. The implausibility of such behaviour has led exponents of the rational expectations school to reject any form of adaptive expectations and to claim that in a non-stochastic environment perfect foresight is the only rational mechanism for the formation of expectations. However the adoption of a nonlinear framework to overcome the dynamic instability problem imposes on perfect foresight models a dynamic behaviour in which there will also be systematic forecast errors.

We believe that the solution to this conundrum lies in the fact that systematic forecast errors are not a function of the expectations mechanism but rather are a quirk of the low order dimensional models that economic theorists are forced to work with in order to maintain mathematical tractability. We have already discussed in this thesis the recent advances in the theory of dynamical systems which indicate that as the dimension of a dynamical system is increased, what appears as a regular periodic motion in lower dimensions turns into that irregular oscillatory motion which has been labelled chaos. So in higher dimensional models economic agents would not observe systematic forecast errors, irrespective of which expectations mechanism they use.

In order to bring out the point that chaotic motion is inherent in the basic model of monetary dynamics we shall analyse a discrete time version of the model. As we saw in the previous chapter with the cobweb model this is the simplest framework in which to observe chaotic behaviour. Our analysis is also appropriate in that the discrete time framework is the more standard one in the literature and we are thereby able to relate the dynamic behaviour referred to above more directly to issues in rational expectations modelling. It is also interesting to note that Burmeister (1980b) has already suggested that the concept of chaos may be relevant for understanding behaviour in economic models when expectations are not convergent. Our principal finding is that the discrete time version of the basic model of monetary dynamics under perfect foresight could indeed display chaotic dynamic behaviour for a wide range of parameter values. The implications of this fact could be profound for the use of rational expectations modelling, since an immediate consequence is that even under the most ideal conditions where a dynamic model is known to economic agents and is subject to no random shocks as it evolves through time, perfect foresight is a practical impossibility. We shall amplify this point in the concluding section.

7.2 **The Basic Nonlinear Model of Monetary Dynamics**

We consider an economy producing one non-durable good and in which there is only one asset, money. The level of homogeneous output is assumed fixed. Since the output is non-durable, saving can only be done through the holding of money. The desired money holding at time t will depend on the expected rate of change of prices. Let M^d, P and π denote respectively the nominal money demand, price of homogeneous output and expected proportionate rate of change of prices, all at time t.

In this simple economy we assume that there is a fixed transactions demand for money which we denote by T. It is the asset demand for money which is of interest and importance in this type of model. Letting A denote the asset demand for real money balances we postulate that a certain fraction of (physical) wealth will be held as real money balances and this fraction will depend on π, i.e., A - $\alpha(\pi)$W, where W represents (physical) wealth remaining after transactions demand has been subtracted from fixed output. Since we are assuming fixed physical output in this model we may henceforth set W - 1. We further postulate that $\alpha'(\pi) < 0$. This is a standard assumption and is usually justified by arguing that as π increases, nominal money holdings lose purchasing power in terms of real physical goods, thus decreasing the asset demand for real money. It is clear that α varies between the limits 1 (all physical wealth held in money) and 0 (no physical wealth held in money). Thus $\alpha(\pi)$ must have the general shape shown in figure 7.1. We have preferred to draw α approaching its upper and lower limits asymptotically since this function is an aggregation of the decisions of many individual agents.

It is also possible to justify the general shape of the function $\alpha(\pi)$ by appealing to a utility maximizing framework. We may postulate the typical economic agent at any point in time as facing the decision problem of how much of physical wealth to consume in the current period and how much to hold as money which may be used to purchase consumption in the next period.

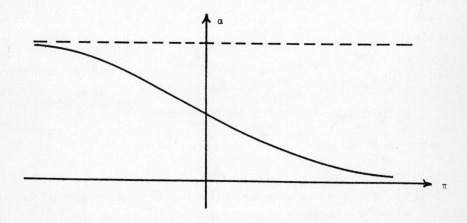

Figure 7.1 Fraction of physical wealth held as real money balances

Summing the transactions demand and asset demand we may write the demand for real money balances as $M^d/P = T + \alpha(\pi)$. Taking logarithms of this latter equation we may write the money demand function as

$$m^d = p + f(\pi), \tag{7.1}$$

where $m^d = \log M^d$, $p = \log P$ and $f(\pi) = \log (T + \alpha(\pi))$.

The function $f(\pi)$ will also have the general shape shown in figure 7.1, but varying between the limits $\log (T + 1)$ ($= f_u$) and $\log T$ ($= f_1$). We shall assume that $f(\pi)$ is close to a linear function over its middle section, in keeping with empirical evidence that over "normal" operating ranges of the independent variable the money demand function is close to linear. It follows that the general shape of $f'(\pi)$ must be as shown in figure 7.2. We put $f'(0) = -a$ ($a > 0$) and we draw $f'(\pi)$ very flat around this value in keeping with our comment that $f(\pi)$ is almost linear over its middle section.

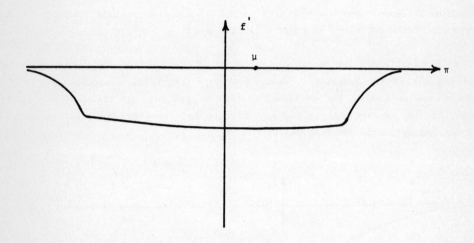

Figure 7.2 Derivative of the money demand function

If expectations are formed adaptively then π and p are related by

$$\dot{\pi} = \frac{1}{\tau}(\dot{p} - \pi), \tag{7.2}$$

where τ is the time lag in the formation of expectations or alternatively, $1/\tau$ is the speed of adjustment of expectations. In the limit as $\tau \to 0^+$, so that there is no lag in the formation of expectations, equation (7.2) reduces to the perfect foresight case

$$\pi = \dot{p}. \tag{7.3}$$

Finally we specify the process of adjustment in the money market. We shall assume a process of lagged adjustment given by the differential equation

$$\dot{p} = \beta(m - p - f(\pi)), \tag{7.4}$$

which shows the rate of price change as a positive linear function of the excess supply of money. Here $\beta(>0)$ is the speed of adjustment and m is the log of the money supply. Equation (7.4) has a long tradition in models of monetary dynamics, see for example Goldman (1972).

The differential equations (7.2) and (7.4) describe the dynamics of the basic model of monetary dynamics. Eliminating p and assuming a money supply growing at the constant rate μ we find that the dynamics of the model are governed by the second order differential equation

$$\frac{\tau}{\beta}\ddot{\pi} + (\frac{1}{\beta} + \tau + f'(\pi))\dot{\pi} + \pi = \mu. \tag{7.5}$$

We denote the equilibrium expected rate of inflation and actual rate of inflation by $\bar{\pi}$, $\dot{p}$ respectively and note that

$$\bar{\pi} = \mu \text{ and } \dot{p} = \bar{\pi}. \tag{7.6}$$

We shall analyse the differential equation (7.5) first in the perfect foresight case when $\tau = 0$ and then take a broader perspective by analysing the adaptive expectations case when $\tau > 0$.

7.3 The Naive Dynamics of the Perfect Foresight Case. $\tau = 0$

Setting $\tau = 0$ in equation (7.5) and rearranging we find that the dynamics of the perfect foresight case are given by

$$\dot{\pi} = \frac{\mu - \pi}{1/\beta + f'(\pi)} . \tag{7.7}$$

In the traditional local linear analysis of equation (7.7) we would put $f'(\pi) = -a$ so that

$$\dot{\pi} = \frac{\mu - \pi}{1/\beta - a} . \tag{7.8}$$

Thus the equilibrium point $(\bar{\pi}, \dot{p})$ (henceforth denoted E) is locally stable if $a < 1/\beta$ and locally unstable if $a > 1/\beta$. We note that Sargent and Wallace assume the money market clears instantaneously so that $\beta \to \infty$. In this case the equilibrium point is always locally unstable. We shall assume that the money market adjusts sufficiently rapidly that $a > 1/\beta$ and hence concentrate on the locally unstable situation. In order to keep the mathematical analysis simple we shall also assume that the rate of monetary expansion μ is such that $f'(\mu) = -a$.

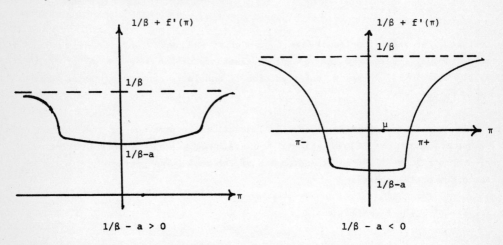

Figure 7.3   The sign of the denominator of equation 7.7

The local instability of the equilibrium point of equation (7.8) contains the genesis of the dynamic instability problem. Unless the initial conditions happen to satisfy $\pi(0) = \bar{\pi}$, $\dot{p}(0) = \dot{p}$ all time paths of π and p are diverging. In order to ensure that the initial conditions are appropriately chosen after a parameter change (e.g. a change in μ) Sargent and Wallace introduce the concept of discontinuous jumps in price. However Burmeister (1980a) claims "....we must be concerned whether or not there exist any economic mechanisms that select initial prices consistent with dynamic stability".

A broader and more interesting picture is obtained if we go beyond the local linear analysis and take account of the nonlinear nature of equation (7.7). The postulated form of $f'(\pi)$ shown in figure 7.2 leads to the graphs of $1/\beta + f'(\pi)$ shown in figure 7.3. We distinguish two cases: (a) $a < 1/\beta$ (the case of local stability) so that $1/\beta + f'(\pi) > 0$ and hence $\dot{\pi} < 0$ for all π. In this case the global qualitative behaviour of the time path of π is as predicted by the local linear analysis, all time paths are tending to the equilibrium point as shown in figure 7.4a. (b) $a > 1/\beta$ (the case of local instability) so that $1/\beta + f'(\pi) \leq 0$ for $\pi_- \leq \pi \leq \pi_+$ and $1/\beta + f'(\pi) > 0$ for all other π (see figure 7.3b). Hence for initial values of π satisfying $\pi_- < \pi(0) < \pi_+$ (but $\pi(0) \neq \mu$) we have $\dot{\pi} > 0$ and π is moving away from the equilibrium point. However, along any such path the limit of $\dot{\pi}$ as $\pi \to \pi_+$ (π_-) is

$+\infty(-\infty)$ and so the lines $\pi = \pi_+$ and $\pi = \pi_-$ are reached in finite time. For initial values satisfying $\pi(0) > \pi_+$ or $\pi(0) < \pi_-$ the dynamic motion is reversed since now $\dot{\pi} < 0$ and the lines $\pi = \pi_+$ and $\pi = \pi_-$ are again reached in finite time. The time path of π from various initial values is shown in figure 7.4b.

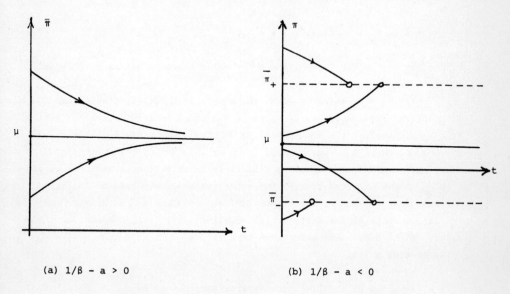

(a) $1/\beta - a > 0$ (b) $1/\beta - a < 0$

<u>Figure 7.4</u> Time paths of π under perfect foresight

In the case which interests us, namely that of local instability when $a > 1/\beta$, the picture obtained by the nonlinear analysis is quite different from that which is normally inferred on the basis of the local linear analysis. Certainly the equilibrium point is unstable but now all time paths satisfying $\pi(0) \neq \mu$ rather than tending to infinity tend to either π_+ or π_-. However, these points are not equilibrium points of the differential equation (7.7), indeed at π_+ and π_- the right hand side of the differential equation (7.7) is infinite.

It is not possible to gain a full understanding of why π apparently "gets stuck" at π_+ or π_- by remaining in the one dimensional framework of equation (7.7). We must rather go to the two dimensional framework of equation (7.5), deduce the behaviour of π implied by this equation and then consider the limit $\tau \to 0^+$. It can be shown mathematically that the qualitative behaviour of equation (7.9) is the same for $\tau = 0$ and $\tau \to 0^+$ and we shall give the appropriate reference at a later point.

7.4 The Dynamics of the Adaptive Expectations Case. $\tau > 0$

In order to transfer the equilibrium point to the origin we define the new variable Π by $\Pi = \pi - \mu$ and express equation (7.5) in the form

$$\frac{\tau}{\beta}\ddot{\pi} + (-\epsilon + f'(\pi + \mu) - f'(\mu))\,\dot{\pi} + \pi = 0, \tag{7.9}$$

where we have set $\epsilon = -f'(\mu) - \tau - 1/\beta = a - \tau - 1/\beta$ since we assume $f'(\mu) = -a$.

It is a relatively routine matter to show the origin is a locally stable equilibrium point of the differential equation (7.9) for $\epsilon < 0$ and a locally unstable equilibrium point for $\epsilon > 0$. These are the same local stability conditions as in the perfect foresight case. Most analyses would stop at this point concluding that when inflationary expectations are adjusting relatively rapidly (i.e. $\epsilon > 0$) the supply of real balances , the expected rate of inflation and hence the rate of inflation are all diverging from equilibrium. However, as we show below a more careful mathematical analysis of the differential equation (7.9) taking account of the non-linear nature of the money demand function reveals that the diverging paths are in fact tending towards a limit cycle.

In fact the eigenvalues of the linearised system turn out to be
$$\lambda_1, \lambda_2 = \beta[\epsilon \pm (\epsilon^2 - 4\tau/\beta)^{1/2}]/2\tau. \tag{7.10}$$

We see from (7.10) that close to the point $\epsilon = 0$, at which local stability turns to local instability, the eigenvalues are complex. Hence close to $\epsilon = 0$ the dynamic motion in the $(\pi, \dot{\pi})$ phase plane must be such that paths are spiralling into the equilibrium for $\epsilon < 0$ and spiralling away from the equilibrium for $\epsilon > 0$. It is a straightforward matter to verify that the conditions of the Hopf bifurcation theorem (i.e. $\lambda(0)$ pure complex and real part of $\lambda'(0) \neq 0$) are satisfied indicating the existence of a limit cycle for either $\epsilon < 0$ or $\epsilon > 0$.

Applying the method of averaging we may investigate the nature of the limit cycle born at the bifurcation point $\epsilon = 0$. Writing (7.9) as a first-order system and using the results of section 2.5 we find that the first order approximation to the amplitude of the limit cycle is given by the solution of the differential equation

$$\dot{\rho} = \beta\rho(\epsilon - h(\rho))/2\tau, \tag{7.11}$$

where the function h is defined by

$$h(\rho) = \frac{1}{\pi} \int_{0}^{2\pi} [f'(\rho \sin \psi + \mu) - f'(\mu)] \cos^2 \psi \, d \psi, \qquad (7.12)$$

and we show in appendix 7.1 that it has the general shape shown in figure 7.5.

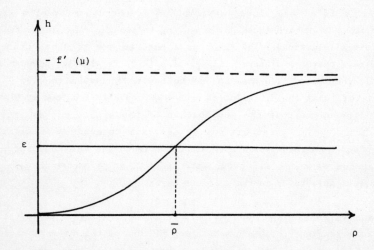

Figure 7.5 The form of $h(\rho)$

When $\epsilon < 0$ the differential equation (7.11) has only one equilibrium point at $\rho = 0$ and since $\dot{\rho} < 0$ for all $\rho > 0$, $\rho(t) \to 0$ as $t \to \infty$ irrespective of the initial values. Thus the qualitative picture obtained from the local linear analysis, namely that equilibrium point E is asymptotically stable when $\epsilon < 0$, continues to be valid in the more general nonlinear case.

When $\epsilon > 0$ the differential equation (7.11) has two equilibrium points. One at $\rho = 0$ and the other at $\rho = \bar{\rho}$ given by

$$h(\bar{\rho}) = \epsilon. \qquad (7.13)$$

Since $\dot{\rho} > 0$ (<0) for $\rho < \bar{\rho}$ (> $\bar{\rho}$), $\rho(t) \to \bar{\rho}$ as $t \to \infty$ irrespective of the initial value of ρ. The local linear analysis in the case $\epsilon > 0$ concentrates on the equilibrium at $\rho = 0$ (i.e. the equilibrium point E) and tells us that this equilibrium point is unstable with $\Pi(t)$ moving away from the origin with increasing oscillations. However, the nonlinear analysis now completes this picture and shows that these oscillations are not unbounded as is sometimes assumed but rather are settling down to a steady oscillation of approximate amplitude $\bar{\rho}$.

As in our applications in earlier chapters the method of averaging enables us to get a feel for the qualitative effects of parameter changes on the amplitude of the limit cycle. The expressions derived in appendix 7.1 indicate that $\bar{p}$ is an increasing function of the speed of adjustment parameters $1/r$ and β but is barely affected by moderate changes in the rate of monetary expansion μ.

It is also possible to give a global description of the dynamics of π without employing any approximation techniques, by appealing to two theorems in the theory of nonlinear differential equations. The first is a theorem due to Olech (1963) and enables us to assert that the differential equation (7.9) is globally asymptotically stable for $\epsilon < 0$. The second is a theorem due to Levinson and Smith (1942) which enables us to assert that the differential equation (7.9) has a unique stable limit cycle for $\epsilon > 0$. The details of the application of these theorems are given in appendix 7.2. Thus the picture obtained by approximate methods is seen to be globally valid, however on this approach we are not able to say very much about the qualitative features of the limit cycle (i.e. effects of parameter changes on the amplitude) as we were able to do in the previous paragraph.

The dual approach which we have adopted here of using approximate methods (in our case the method of averaging) to obtain a detailed picture of the dynamics close to a bifurcation point and then using general theorems to obtain a less detailed global picture of the dynamics is really as far as we can carry the analysis of the type of model given the current state of the art in the theory of nonlinear differential equations, however we have already greatly extended the results obtained from the traditional local linear analysis.

Before concluding this section it is worth explaining the operation of the limit cycle motion through an intuitive argument based on the underlying economic assumptions of the model.

We assume that inflationary expectations are adjusting relatively rapidly (i.e. $\epsilon > 0$) so that the equilibrium is locally unstable. Let us start from a situation in which π is above $\bar{\pi}$ and increasing so that eventually the money demand function tends to its lower limit f_1, the expected rate of inflation eventually becoming so large as to reduce the demand for money to the constant level of transactions demand. The continual increase in π leads to a continual increase in the rate of inflation, $\dot{p}$, via equation (7.2). Given that the nominal money supply is growing at a fixed rate, this means that eventually the supply of real balances must start to decline; since if we set $y = \log(M^S/P)$ then $\dot{y} = \mu - \dot{p}$. Since the demand for real balances is "stuck" around f_1, the supply of real balances must eventually drop below the demand, at which point $\dot{\pi}$ becomes < 0 and so π starts to decrease. As π continues to decrease the demand for real balances will approach the upper limit f_u.

The continual decline in π means that $\dot{p}$ will eventually fall below the constant growth rate of nominal money supply, so that $\dot{y}$ becomes positive and y (and hence the supply of real balances) starts to increase again. Since demand for real balances is "stuck" around f_u, the increase in the supply of real balances eventually creates an excess supply in the money market which eventually leads to $\dot{\pi} > 0$ and the cycle then repeats itself. The bounds on the money demand function combined with the dynamics of the inflationary process prevent a situation in which, in the case of local instability, there is permanent divergence between supply and demand in the money market. This is essentially the economic mechanism which leads the model to exhibit a limit cycle in this case.

7.5 Adaptive Expectations as $\tau \to 0^+$

A major objective of our analysis is to determine what happens to the limit cycle as $\tau \to 0^+$. When $\tau = 0$ the second derivative term in equation (7.9) vanishes and we are left with the differential equation of the perfect foresight model. Lasalle (1949) proves that for a class of second order differential equations, of which (7.9) is a special type, the qualitative behaviour is the same for τ small and positive as for $\tau = 0$. The mathematical arguments used by Lasalle are extremely technical so for the purposes of the present discussion we shall give a heuristic argument which enables us to see quite clearly what happens to the solutions of equation (7.9) as $\tau \to 0^+$.

If we define a new variable Y by

$$\Pi = \dot{Y}, \tag{7.14}$$

it is possible to reduce the differential equation (7.9) to the form

$$\frac{\tau}{\beta} \ddot{Y} + (\tau + 1/\beta) \dot{Y} + f(\dot{Y} + \mu) + Y = 0. \tag{7.15}$$

The mathematical details of this transformation are given in appendix 7.3. In order to analyse the second order differential equation using phase plane techniques we write it as the first order system.

$$\tau \dot{\Pi} = -\beta[(\tau + 1/\beta) \Pi + f(\Pi + \mu) + Y], \tag{7.16a}$$

$$\dot{Y} = \Pi. \tag{7.16.}$$

The slope of phase trajectories in the (Π,Y) phase plane is given by

$$\frac{d\Pi}{dY} = - \frac{\beta[(\tau + 1/\beta)\ \Pi + f(\Pi + \mu) + Y]}{\tau\Pi}. \qquad (7.17)$$

For $\tau \rightarrow 0^+$ this slope is almost infinite (and is infinite when $\tau = 0$) except in those regions of the phase plane where

$$(\tau + 1/\beta)\ \Pi + f(\Pi + \mu) + Y = 0. \qquad (7.18)$$

The graph of this last relationship is labelled FF' in figure 7.6, details of this construction are given in appendix 7.3.

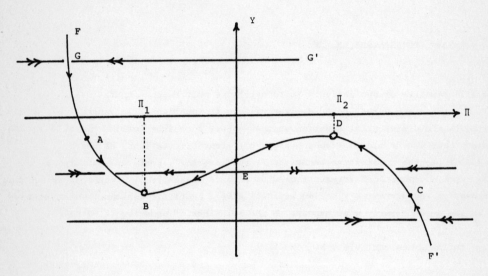

<u>Figure 7.6</u> Regions of fast and slow motion in the (Π, Y) phase plane

The phase plane may be considered as divided into two regions. The first, consisting of the whole phase plane excluding the curve FF' and a small neighbourhood about it, is the region of "fast motion". In this region $d\Pi/dY$ and $\dot{\Pi}$ are almost infinite so that phase trajectories are almost horizontal with Y barely changing and Π changing very rapidly in a jump-wise fashion. By considering the sign of $(\tau + 1/\beta)\pi + f(\pi + \mu) + Y$ above and below the curve FF' we are able to give the directions of change of Π in the fast region as shown in figure 7.6 by the horizontal lines which represent the limiting case $\tau = 0$ e.g. the path G'G. In the fast region the equations of motion are given approximately by

$$Y = Y^o = \text{const.}, \qquad (7.19a)$$

$$\dot{\Pi} = -\frac{\beta}{\tau} \left[(\tau + 1/\beta) \, \Pi + f(\Pi + \mu) + Y^o \right]. \tag{7.19b}$$

The second region, consisting of the curve FF′ and a neighbourhood about it, is the region of "slow motion". In this region $\dot{\Pi}$ is no longer close to infinity since $(\tau + 1/\beta) \, \Pi + f(\Pi + \mu) + Y \approx 0$. In the slow region the equations of motion are given approximately by

$$(\tau + 1/\beta)\Pi + f(\Pi + \mu) + Y = 0, \tag{7.20a}$$

and

$$\dot{Y} = \pi, \tag{7.20b}$$

which are the equations of motion along the curve FF′. Taking account of the sign of Π and the slope of FF′ we obtain the directions of the motion along FF′ as shown in figure 7.6. Whatever the initial value in the slow region, motion is towards either the point B or the point D.

The curve FF′ is in fact the one-dimensional manifold on which the dynamics of the perfect foresight model as analysed in section 7.3 occur. The point E is the equilibrium of the perfect foresight model. Whatever the initial values, motion of Π is either towards D (the equivalent of the point π_+ in figure 7.4b) or towards the point B (the equivalent of the point π_- in figure 7.4b). The question that we were unable to answer using the framework of section 7.3 was how can the time paths of π be tending to points which are not equilibrium points of the governing differential equation? With the one-dimensional manifold FF′ now embedded in the two-dimensional (Π,Y) phase plane we are able to answer that question. The direction of motion from the points B or D is into the region of fast motion. Thus Π, from the point B, jumps almost instantaneously to the point C and from the point D jumps almost instantaneously to the point A. In fact in the limit $\tau = 0$ these jumps are instantaneous. Thus, supposing $\tau = 0$ and starting form the point I in figure 7.7, Π moves along FF′ to the point D then jumps instantaneously to the point A on FF′, motion is then along FF′ to the point B from which ℓ jumps instantaneously to the point C on FF′, motion is then along FF′ to the point D from which the cycle repeats itself. The cycle $D \rightarrow A \rightarrow B \rightarrow C \rightarrow D \rightarrow \ldots$ is the limiting limit cycle of the differential equation 7.9. The time path for Π along the limiting limit cycle is shown in figure 7.8. On the limiting limit cycle Π oscillates between the limits Π_u and Π_1 which are determined respectively by the points C and A on the curve FF′.

From an arbitrary initial point I′ in figure 7.7 and for $\tau \approx 0^+$, Π will jump almost instantaneously to the region of slow motion in a neighbourhood of the curve FF′ and then proceed to a neighbourhood of the point B. From B motion is again into the fast

region so that Π jumps almost instantaneously to the slow region in a neighbourhood
of the point C, motion is then along the slow region until a neighbourhood of point D
is reached, from which motion is almost instantaneous to the point A and then another
cycle is performed towards a limit cycle which is closer to the limiting limit cycle
the closer is r to zero.

We are now able to paint the total picture obtained from the nonlinear analysis. The
adaptive expectations model with $r \approx 0^+$ has a locally unstable equilibrium point, but
all time paths of π (and p) move towards a stable limit cycle. In the perfect
foresight limit when $r - 0$, the stable limit cycle becomes the stable limiting limit
cycle ABCD of figure 7.7 with the time path of Π being the regular periodic motion
shown in figure 7.8. On one cycle of this motion Π increases monotonically from Π_ℓ
to Π_1 then jumps instantaneously up to Π_u , decreases monotonically to Π_2, jumps
instantaneously down to Π_ℓ and the the cycle repeats itself. For the original
variable π the motion just described is relative to the horizontal line $\pi - \bar{\pi} - \mu$.
The stable limit cycle ABCD is approached from any initial conditions and its
amplitude is determined by Π_u and Π_ℓ.

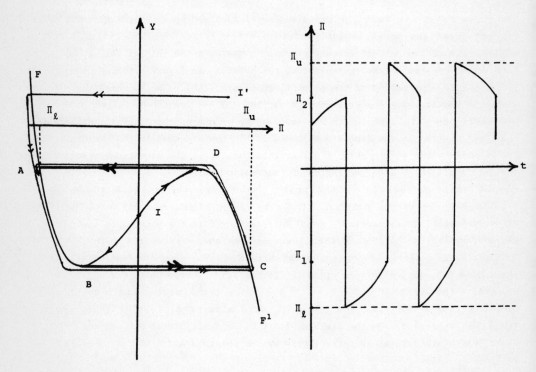

Figure 7.7 The limiting limit   **Figure 7.8** The time path of Π
        cycle ABCD   on ABCD

In the nonlinear framework which we have described the problem of an appropriate choice of initial conditions, which is the characteristic of the dynamic instability problem referred to in section 7.1, does not arise. Now whatever the initial conditions the stable limit cycle is approached and the instantaneous changes in π (and hence in p) arise naturally as a result of the existence of the regions of fast and slow motion. Also in this framework we see that there is a natural transition from adaptive expectations to perfect foresight as $\tau \to 0^+$ with there being no fundamental difference in qualitative behaviour between a small lag in expectations and zero lag in expectations.

Our analysis has demonstrated that the dynamics of perfect foresight (PF) models is better understood by adopting a nonlinear framework and viewing perfect foresight as the limit of adaptive expectations (AE) when the expectations time lag tends to zero. Indeed PF and AE must have the same qualitative behaviour when the expectations time lag is small. The approach we adopt allows the manifold upon which the dynamics of PF occurs to be embedded in a higher dimension. The division of the phase space in this higher dimension into regions of fast and slow motion quite naturally allows jump-wise changes in the economic variables. When PF models are viewed from the lower dimension as in most traditional analyses the jump-wise changes seem to be arbitrarily imposed. The seemingly perverse stability behaviour associated with PF models such as the dynamic instability problem no longer seems perverse when viewed from the higher dimension of AE models. It is not only the addition of another dimension which allows us to overcome the dynamic instability problem but also, and more importantly, the use of a nonlinear model. The nonlinear model introduces an additional stable equilibrium concept, namely stable limit cycles, so that the existence of locally unstable equilibrium points is no longer incompatible with an overall stable equilibrium situation.

The current wisdom in macro-economics would criticise the use of adaptive expectations in the model we have analysed on the grounds that economic agents would perceive the limit cycle and hence perceive that prediction errors were a regular periodic motion and would change their adaptive expectations to perfect foresight. However, when we adopt the nonlinear viewpoint this argument does not stand up since, as we have seen, the perfect foresight model also exhibits limit cycle behaviour, and in fact, the qualitative behaviour of the dynamics of the model is the same under both expectations mechanisms. More importantly a real world continuous time model would have dimensions greater than two and as we have pointed out in chapter two, in higher dimensional models economic agents will not always see regular periodic motion but rather chaotic or stochastic motion from which they are never able to deduce the underlying deterministic model.

To demonstrate that the mechanism for the generation of chaotic behaviour is present in the monetary dynamics model under perfect foresight we shall in the next section analyse a discrete time version of the model.

7.6 The Discrete Time Model of Monetary Dynamics

Using the subscript t to denote the value of a variable in time period t we write the discrete time version of the money demand equation (7.1) as

$$m_t^d - p_t = f(\pi_t). \tag{7.21}$$

In this discussion we shall assume that the money supply is constant over time i.e.

$$m_t^s = m, \tag{7.22}$$

so that the process of lagged adjustment in the money market may be written

$$p_{t+1} - p_t = \alpha(m - m_t^d), \qquad \alpha > 0, \tag{7.23}$$

as in Burmeister (1980a, b).

Upon use of (7.21) this last equation becomes

$$p_{t+1} = \alpha m + (1 - \alpha)p_t - \alpha f(\pi_t), \tag{7.24}$$

which is a difference equation expressing the price in period $(t + 1)$ as a function of the price and expected price change in the previous period.

The model is closed by specifying a mechanism for the formation of expectations. If we assume perfect foresight then we would have

$$\pi_t = p_{t+1} - p_t. \tag{7.25}$$

Equations (7.24-25) specify the dynamics of the perfect foresight model since (7.25) may be used to eliminate π_t in equation (7.24). Notice that if we assume the traditional linear form $f(\pi) = b - a\pi$ (a>0) for the money demand function then (7.24-25) combine to yield the linear difference equation

$$p_{t+1} = \frac{\alpha(m - b)}{1 - \alpha a} + (1 - \frac{\alpha}{1 - \alpha a})p_t, \tag{7.26}$$

which is effectively the difference equation discussed by Burmeister (1980a, eqn. 7.3.12) in the case of constant money supply. The necessary and sufficient condition that the equilibrium $\bar{p} = (m - b)$ be stable, and hence that the equilibrium of the general nonlinear system (7.24-25) be locally stable, is that

$$0 < \alpha < \frac{2}{1 + 2a} . \tag{7.27}$$

When the speed of adjustment in the money market is such that this condition is violated i.e. $\alpha > 2/(1 + 2a)$, then, if we remain within the framework of the linear difference equation (7.26), the only way for prices to be convergent is for the initial value of price to jump so as to satisfy $p_0 = \bar{p}$ and so that hence $p_t = \bar{p}$ for all subsequent time. Even if one is prepared to accept the arbitrary jump in initial conditions, Burmeister (1980a) points out that the resulting time path $p_t = \bar{p}$ leads to contradictions in a stochastic environment when the linear difference equation (7.26) has a stochastic disturbance term appended to it.

After eliminating p_t between equations (7.24-25) we find that π_t satisfies the first-order difference equation

$$V(\pi_{t+1}) = U(\pi_t), \tag{7.28}$$

where the functions V and U are defined by

$$V(\pi) = \pi + \alpha f(\pi), \tag{7.29}$$

and

$$U(\pi) = (1 - \alpha)\pi + \alpha f(\pi). \tag{7.30}$$

The difference equation (7.28) is an implicit equation for π_{t+1} and may be put into the conventional form by inverting the function V i.e.

$$\pi_{t+1} = F(\pi_t) = V^{-1} (U(\pi_t)). \tag{7.31}$$

In order to determine the general form of the nonlinear function F we need first to understand the forms of the functions V and U. These functions are sketched in figures 7.9 and 7.10 respectively, according to the analysis outlined in appendix 7.4. The salient features of the graphs of these functions are (i) the function V is monotonic increasing for $\alpha < 1/a$, has a maximum then a minimum for $\alpha > 1/a$ and is asymptotic to the lines $\pi + f_u$ and $\pi + f_\ell$, and (ii) the function U is monotonic increasing for $\alpha < 1/(1 + a)$, has a maximum then a minimum for $1/(1 + a) < \alpha < 1$, is

118

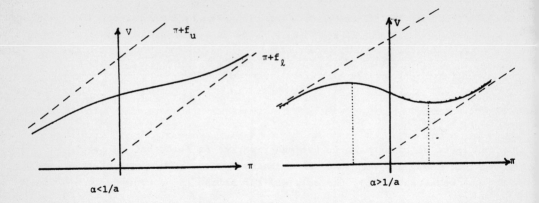

Figure 7.9 The function V

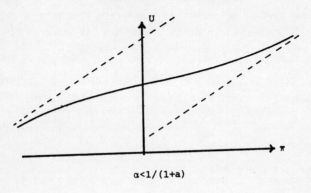

Figure 7.10 The function U

monotonic decreasing for $\alpha > 1$ and in every case is asymptotic to the lines $(1 - \alpha)\pi + \alpha f_u$ and $(1 - \alpha)\pi + \alpha f_\ell$.

In appendix 7.5 we give the details of construction of the function F ($\equiv V^{-1} o \ U$) whose graph is displayed in figures 7.11 (a) and (b). We note the following features of the function F:-

(a)   For $0 < \alpha < 1/(1 + a)$, monotonic increasing and slope < 1. In this case the mapping F displays both local and global stability; global stability following from the asymptotic behaviour of F. (Figure 7.11a)

(b)   For $1/(1 + a) < \alpha < 1/a$ F has a maximum at u_1 and a minimum at u_2. On the subinterval $1/(1 + a) < \alpha < 1/(0.5 + a)$ the origin continues to be locally and globally stable, whilst on the subinterval $1/(0.5 + a) < \alpha < 1/a$ the origin is locally unstable. (Figure 7.11b)

The function F for the parameter range $\alpha > 1/a$ becomes multivalued since the functions U and V both have multivalued inverses in this range. It is not clear how to obtain the correct single valued map for F in this case if we remain in the framework of the discrete time model given by equations (7.21-23 and 7.25) which was our starting point. It seems that the appropriate single valued map should have the features displayed in figures appropriate single valued map should have the features displayed in figures 7.11 (c) and (d). We have arrived at these figures by discretizing the differential equation model of Section 7.5 and using our knowledge of the behaviour of the limiting limit cycle, figure 7.7, and the behaviour that this imposes on the dynamics of π_t. (See appendix 7.6). Our understanding of the differential equation model was obtained by analysing the two-dimensional model in which there was lagged adjustment both of expectations and in the money market and then considering the limit $r \to 0^+$. Similarly, in order to properly analyse the discrete time model we would need to consider the two-dimensional model by replacing the perfect foresight relationship of equation (7.5) with the adaptive expectations equation:

$$\pi_t \ = \ (1 - r)(p_{t+1} - p_t) + r\pi_{t-1}, \ (0 \le r \le 1)$$

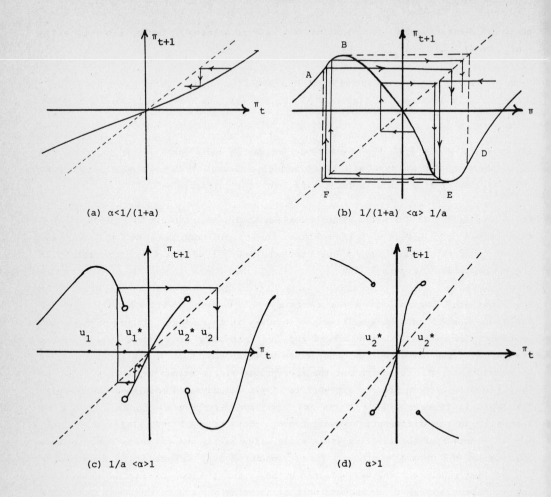

(a) $\alpha < 1/(1+a)$

(b) $1/(1+a) < \alpha > 1/a$

(c) $1/a < \alpha > 1$

(d) $\alpha > 1$

Figure 7.11 The function F

and considering the limit $r \to 0^+$. Unfortunately such an analysis for the resulting two-dimensional difference equation model, does not follow as simply as for the two-dimensional differential equation model since it is not possible to use phase plane analysis as we did for the differential equation model. A proper anlaysis of the two-dimensional difference equation model would require a computer simulation analysis of the type used by Guckenheimer, Oster and Ipaktchi (1977) to analyse two-dimensional maps in models of population dynamics. Such an alysis would certainly be worthwhile but would take us beyond the goals we have set for this thesis. However, we are able to make the main point which we wish to bring out about the discrete time model by reference to figure (7.11b).

Let us now discuss the dynamic behaviour of map $\pi_{t+1} = F(\pi_t)$. As we have already pointed out the equilibrium point at the origin is locally and globally stable for $0 < \alpha < 1/(0.5 + a)$. For the purposes of our discussion, in the set $1/(0.5 + a) < \alpha < 1/a$ the map F displays all relevant dynamic behaviour. In this set the origin becomes locally unstable, however, the general shape of F ensures that for large π_t trajectories are moving toward the origin. In fact all trajectories are ultimately attracted into and cannot escape from the region ABCDEF in figure 7.11b. Clearly all trajectories are exhibiting bounded oscillatory motion and what we would like to further investigate is whether this oscillatory motion is periodic or chaotic.

In chapter 6 we discussed the parabolic map $x_{t+1} = \lambda x_t(1 - x_t)$ in relation to the cobweb model. The characteristic feature of this map was the period doubling of oscillatory orbits around the non-zero equilibrium point as λ increases, with chaotic behaviour appearing once a critical value of λ is passed. Our application of these results to the cobweb model relied on the fact that this behaviour is a universal characteristic of all single hump maps. It will be noted that the map contained in the window ABCDEF of figure 7.11b and which ultimately determines the behaviour of all trajectories is double humped.

The behaviour of the double hump map has recently been studied by May (1983) who analyses the cubic map $x_{t+1} = \lambda x_t(ax_t^2+1-a)$. This analysis indicates that, as with the single hump parabolic map, trajectories around the unstable equilibrium point can exhibit a cascade of period doubling with chaos eventually emerging. However this fact has not yet been established as has been the case with the quadratic map. The matter is still the subject of current research in dynamical systems theory. Even once this result is established it would still remain to show that the dynamic behaviour is universal i.e. that all double hump maps behave like the cubic map.

In order to establish the possibility of chaotic behaviour we shall consider an explicit functional form for the nonlinear demand function f and then calculate the

Lyapunov characteristic exponent of the resulting map F. If from an initial point π_0 we calculate the trajectory (π_i: i=1...N) then the Lyapunov exponent is defined as

$$\sigma(\pi_0) = \lim_{n \to \infty} \frac{1}{n} \sum_{t=1}^{n} \ln|F'(\pi_t)|. \tag{7.32}$$

It can be shown that except for a set of measure zero, σ is independent of the initial point π_0. Essentially σ measures the mean exponential rate of divergence of two initially close trajectories and so $\sigma > 0$ indicates chaotic orbits whilst $\sigma < 0$ indicates that orbits are being attracted to a stable periodic orbit. Another important property of σ is that it is independent of the specific form in which the map is written. In other words if G is another map obtained from F by an invertible coordinate transformation (and hence has the same qualitative shape as F) then G has the same Lyapunov exponent as F. Thus the investigation of the behaviour of σ for a particular map is indicative of the behaviour of σ for a whole family of maps. An account of Lyapunov exponents is given by Lichtenberg and Lieberman (1983).

The function f given by the formula $f(x) = c - b \arctan(x - d)$, (b>0, c>b$\pi$/2) has all the properties of the money demand function under consideration. In figure 7.12 we plot the Lyapunov exponent for the corresponding map F over the parameter range $1/(1+a) < \alpha < 1/a$. For this calculation we took c=11,b=10, d=0.2 and N=100000; the α interval was divided into 600 points. We see from figure 7.12 that σ does become positive over certain intervals of α, indicating that trajectories of F follow chaotic orbits for these values of α.

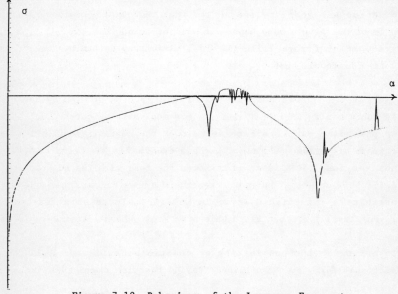

Figure 7.12 Behaviour of the Lyapunov Exponent

7.7 **Discussion**

The picture of the nonlinear model of monetary dynamics which we have now constructed shows that the limit cycle of the continuous time formulation, which emerges as local stability turns to local instability can manifest itself as chaotic behaviour in the discrete time formulation. So the regular periodic motion of the limit cycle which is often seen as unrealistic due to its predictability is replaced by the irregular oscillatory motion of chaotic behaviour which as we discuss below is not predictable.

The discrete time nonlinear model which we have analysed is in its linearised form the deterministic version of the model used by Burmeister (1980a,b) to point up many of the stability problems of models of monetary dynamics. As we have already pointed out in connection with the continuous time model the nonlinear framework does not give rise to the same instability problems, in the case of local instability solutions are either tending towards periodic paths or are displaying chaotic behaviour.

We have already pointed out that the simple model that we have analysed here is the basic mechanism causing the saddle point instability in a wide range of dynamic economic models. For instance the Tobin models - Tobin (1965) and Hadjimichalakis (1971) - and models of exchange rate dynamics - Gray and Turnovsky (1979), all have as the root cause of their saddle point instability the mechanism which we have analysed. In all of these models a nonlinearity of the type we have used can be justified and introduced quite naturally. As we have seen the effect of the nonlinearitiy is to contain the motion on the locally unstable manifold. For other classes of models (i.e. not of the monetary dynamics type) which also display saddle point instability, such as that of Blanchard (1981), it should also be possible to find nonlinearities which will have the same effect on the dynamic behaviour. This remains the task of future research with the principal task of the economic theorist being to find and justify those nonlinearities which are most plausible for the class of model at hand.

For the purposes of our discussion an important question is to know whether the type of dynamic behaviour we have observed is simply a feature of the simple, low dimensional model that we have used . Can we expect to observe the same dynamic behaviour as we put the basic mechanism of the nonlinear money demand function into higher dimensional models which might include more difference or differential equations to cater for additional factors such as capital accumulation and a more elaborate financial sector? Recent advances in the theory of dynamical systems indicate a definite yes to this question; see e.g. Guckenheimer and Holmes (1983) and Orsag and McLaughlin (1980). What emerges from this literature is that as the dimension of the dynamical system increases chaotic behaviour is more likely to be the norm. Furthermore the higher the dimension of the system the weaker the form of nonlinearity required to generate such behaviour. For example the celebrated Lorenz equations which gave much impetus to the study of chaotic phenomena and the Rossler (1976) equations are examples of three dimensional differential equations which are linear except for some simple quadratic nonlinearities but which exhibit chaotic behaviour for wide parameter ranges.

A noted characteristic of chaotic behaviour is that solutions from nearby initial values do not stay close together as time evolves. This in fact is the significance of the positivity of the Lyapunov exponent which measure the mean rate of exponential divergence of nearby solutions. A positive Lyapunov exponent indicates that nearby solutions are moving apart exponentially rapidly. A consequence of this characterictic is that in their chaotic regions deterministic nonlinear models exhibit unpredictable stochastic behaviour. This is so since we can never know initial values precisely but only within some band of measurement error. Certainly with economic data this band could be quite wide. Since different initial values within this measurement error band yield entirely different time paths predictability in such models becomes impossible except in a world where initial values are known with infinite precision.

The lack of predictability in deterministic nonlinear models must have some ramifications for one of the basic tenets of rational expectations theory. This theory holds that rational economic agents, given the economic model, will predict values of economic variables that will, on average, equal their expectations. Their expectations diverge from actual realised values only because of exogenous random shocks (e.g. authorities randomly varying the money supply). If there were no exogenous shocks then the economic agents would have perfect foresight. What our discussion reveals is that even if economic agents do know the model, and there are various theories to explain how they might e.g. Bray (1983), and there are no exogenous random shocks the agents would not be able to accurately predict the future course of the economy due to the uncertainty in initial values. It is perhaps worth pointing out that in addition to the uncertainty in initial values the economic agents would only possess estimates of the parameters of the model and these estimates would also be only known within some error band. This "fuzziness" in the parameters of the model will compound the lack of predictability problem that the economic agents face.

If economic agents are not able to predict the future course of economic variables under the ideal conditions when exogenous random shocks are absent then they will not be able to determine the average opinion which is supposed to be generated endogenously by the model. The indeterminacy of the average opinion implies that even

if the agents were to know the parameters of the stochastic process driving the
exogenous random shocks they would not be able to calculate the objective probability
distribution of outcomes. The assumption that agents can calculate this probability
distribution is the essence of the rational expectations hypothesis.

Appendix 7.1

Consider the function h defined by equation 7.12. Note first of all that,

(i) $h(0) = 0,$

(ii) $\lim\limits_{\rho \to \infty} h(\rho) = - \dfrac{f'(\mu)}{\pi} \displaystyle\int_0^{2\pi} \cos^2 \psi \, d\psi = - f'(\mu)$

(iii) $h'(\rho) = \dfrac{1}{\rho} \displaystyle\int_0^{2\pi} f''(\rho \sin \psi + \mu) \sin \psi \cos^2 \psi \, d\psi$

From the general sketch of $f'(\pi)$ displayed in fig 7.2. we obtain for $f''(\pi)$ the sketch displayed in figure 7A1.   We see that f'' is significantly different from zero only for those values of π where $f(\pi)$ is highly non-linear. thus the value of $h'(\rho)$ is determined by the humped values of $f''(\pi)$ in figure 7A1.   At the negative, left-hand hump $\rho \sin \psi + \mu < 0$, so that $\sin \psi < 0$ and so this hump gives a positive contribution to $h'(\rho)$. At the positive right-hand hump, the major contribution to the integral comes from the region where $f'' > 0$ and $\sin \psi > 0$, so that on balance, this hump also gives a positive contribution to $h'(\rho)$.   Thus we assert that

(iv) $h'(\rho) > 0$, and $h'(0) = 0.$

and

(v) $\lim\limits_{\rho \to \infty} h'(\rho) = 0.$

The properties (i) to (v) allow us to give the sketch of h displayed in figure 7.5.

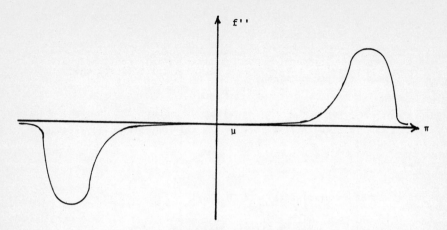

<u>Figure 7A1</u> Form of $f''(\pi)$

The qualitative features of the amplitude $\bar{\rho}$ are obtained by implicitly differentiating equation (7.13). Thus we have

$$\frac{\partial \bar{\rho}}{\partial \tau} = \frac{1}{h(\bar{\rho})} \frac{\partial \epsilon}{\partial \tau} = -1/h'(\rho) < 0,$$

$$\frac{\partial \bar{\rho}}{\partial \beta} = \frac{1}{h'(\bar{\rho})} \frac{\partial \epsilon}{\partial \beta} = \frac{1}{h'(\rho)\beta}2 \geq 0,$$

$$\frac{\partial \rho}{\partial \mu} = \frac{1}{h'(\bar{\rho})} \frac{\partial \epsilon}{\partial \mu} = \frac{-f''(\mu)}{h'(\bar{\rho})}$$

Since we have made the assumption that μ falls on or close to the flat part of $f'(\pi)$, it follows that $\partial \bar{\rho}/\partial \mu \approx 0$. If we drop the assumption that $f'(\pi)$ is perfectly flat over its middle section then at most $\partial \bar{\rho}/\partial \mu$ is small and negative. Either way the amplitude of the limit cycle is barely affected by moderate changes in the rate of monetary expansion.

Appendix 7.2

Note that by setting $Z = \dot{\Pi}$ we may write equation (7.9) as the system

$$\dot{\Pi} = Z = F_1(\Pi, Z),$$

$$\dot{Z} = -\beta(-\epsilon + f'(\Pi + \mu) - f'(\mu))Z)/\tau - \Pi = F_2(\Pi,Z).$$

We state our main results concerning the stability of this non-linear differential system in the following two propositions:

Proposition 1: In the case $\epsilon < 0$ the equilibrium point $(0,0)$ of the above non-linear differential system is globally asymptotically stable.

Proof: Note that

$$Q_1 = \partial F_1/\partial \Pi + \partial F_2/\partial Z = \beta[\epsilon + f'(\mu) - f'(\Pi + \mu)]/\tau.$$

Recall that $-a$ is the lowest value of $f'(\Pi)$ and if we further assume that μ satisfies $f'(\mu) = -a$ then we have by the conditions of the proposition that $Q_1 \leq \epsilon < 0$.

Next we note that

$$Q_2 = \partial F_1/\partial \Pi . \partial F_2/\partial Z - \partial F_1/\partial Z . \partial F_2/\partial \Pi = \beta/\tau > 0$$

and also that

$$Q_3 = \partial F_1/\partial Z . \partial F_2/\partial \Pi = \beta[f''(\Pi + \mu)Z - 1]/\tau \neq 0.$$

Thus all the sufficient conditions given by Olech (1963) (namely, $Q_1 < 0$, $Q_2 > 0$ and $Q_3 \neq 0$ everywhere) for the global asymptotic stability of the equilibrium point are satisfied. This terminates the proof of proposition 1.

Proposition 2: In the case $\epsilon > 0$, the non-linear differential system (7.9) has a unique stable limit cycle.

Proof: We rewrite equation (7.9) in the form

$$\ddot{\Pi} + u(\Pi)\dot{\Pi} + v(\Pi) = 0, \qquad\qquad (*)$$

where $u(\Pi) = \beta[-\epsilon + f'(\Pi + \mu) - f'(\mu)]/\tau$ and $v(\Pi) = \beta\Pi/\tau$. Equation (*) is of the Lienard type discussed for example by Gandolfo (1980) who states a version of the theorem of Levinson and Smith (1942) according to which the above second order nonlinear differential equation has a unique limit cycle if the following conditions are satisfied:- (i) $u(\Pi)$ and $v(\Pi)$ are differentiable, (ii) there exists two positive numbers π_1, π_2 such that $u(\Pi) < 0$, for $-\pi_1 < \Pi < \pi_2$ and $u(\Pi) > 0$ otherwise, (iii) $\Pi\, v(\Pi) > 0$ for $\Pi \neq 0$, and (iv) $U(\Pi)$, $V(\Pi) \to \infty$ as $\Pi \to \infty$, where $U(\Pi) = \int_0^{\Pi} u(s)ds$ and $V(\Pi) = \int_0^{\Pi} v(s)ds$.

It is a relatively simple matter to verify that all of these conditions are satisfied. The crucial condition is (ii) which, given the assumed form of $f'(\Pi)$, is certainly satisfied for $\epsilon > 0$.

The stability of the limit cycle follows by considering the local linearisation of equation (7.9) around $\Pi = 0$, which as we have already seen displays phase curves moving away from the origin when $\epsilon > 0$. Then we consider equation (7.9) for large Π (when $f'(\Pi) = 0$) and we find that it has phase curves moving towards the origin. We thus establish that the phase curves of equation (7.9) move away from the origin for small Π and towards the origin for large Π. Hence the unique limit cycle is stable. This completes the proof of proposition 2.

Appendix 7.3

Setting $\Pi = \dot{Y}$ equation (7.9) becomes.

$$\frac{\tau}{\beta} \ddot{Y} + (-\epsilon + f'(\dot{Y} + \mu) - f'(\mu)) \dot{Y} + \dot{Y} = 0 \qquad (A1)$$

Integrating with respect to time t and observing that
$\int(-\epsilon + f'(\dot{Y} + \mu) - f'(\mu)) \dot{Y} \, dt = \int(-\epsilon + f'(\dot{Y} + \mu) - f'(\mu)) \, d\dot{Y} = -(\epsilon + f'(\mu))\dot{Y} + f(\dot{Y} + \mu)$ we reduce the differential equation (A1) to the differential equation

$$\frac{\tau}{\beta} \ddot{Y} + (\tau + 1/\beta) \dot{Y} + f(\dot{Y} + \mu) + Y = 0, \qquad (A2)$$

which is differential equation (7.15) of the main text.

Referring to equation (7.18) we seek to graph Y as a function of Π given that

$$(\tau + 1/\beta) \Pi + f(\Pi + \mu) + Y = 0.$$

Given the assumptions on the function f we see that as $\Pi \to +\infty$,
$Y \to -(\tau + 1/\beta)\Pi - f_1$ and as $\Pi \to -\infty$, $Y \to -(\tau + 1/\beta)\Pi - f_u$.

The slope of the graph is given by

$$\frac{dY}{d\Pi} = -(\tau + 1/\beta) - f'(\Pi + \mu), \qquad (A3)$$

so that any turning points are given by the roots of the equation

$$\tau + 1/\beta + f'(\Pi + \mu) = 0. \tag{A4}$$

The roots of this last equation are found by constructing a diagram completely analogous to figure 7.3b. Given that τ is small equation (A4) has two roots Π_1 and Π_2 located respectively in a neighbourhood of the points π_- and π_+ of figure 7.3a. The location of the roots Π_1 and Π_2 is illustrated in figure 7A2. By setting $\tau = 0$ in figure 7A2, we obtain figure 7.3b. Note that in order to obtain two roots we must assume $\tau + 1/\beta - a > 0$, however this condition is satisfied given that we are investigating the case of local instability for which $\epsilon > 0$.

After verifying that

$$\frac{dY}{d\Pi} = \begin{array}{l} < 0 \text{ for } \Pi < \Pi_1, \ \Pi > \Pi_2, \\ > 0 \text{ for } \Pi_1 < \Pi < \Pi_2, \end{array}$$

we are able to deduce the sketch given in figure 7.6.

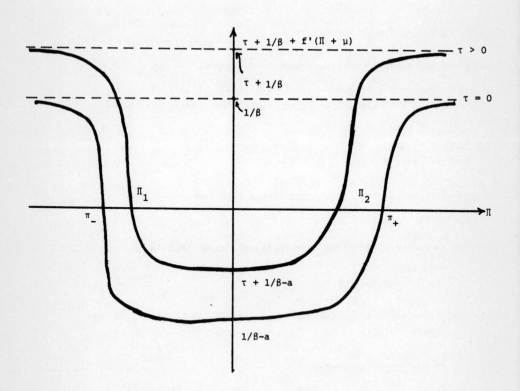

<u>Figure 7A2</u> Location of the roots π_1, π_2

Appendix 7.4

(a) <u>The sketch of V</u>

Since $\lim_{\pi \to \infty} f(\pi) = f_\ell$ and $\lim_{\pi \to \infty} f(\pi) = f_u$ we readily see that $V(\pi)$ is asymptotic to $\pi + f_\ell$ as $\pi \to \infty$ and to $\pi + f_u$ as $\pi \to -\infty$. The slope of V is given by

$$V'(\pi) = 1 + \alpha \, f'(\pi)$$

which is > 0 for $\alpha < 1/a$.

The turning points of V are the roots of

$$f'(\pi) = -\frac{1}{\alpha},$$

which has two roots v_1, v_2 when $\alpha > 1/a$ and no roots for $\alpha < 1/a$.

(b) <u>The sketch of U</u>

Again from the asymptotic behaviour of f we see that

$$U(\pi) \simeq (1 - \alpha)\pi + \alpha \, f_u \qquad \text{as } \pi \to -\infty,$$

and

$$U(\pi) \simeq (1 - \alpha)\pi + \pi \, f_\ell \qquad \text{as } \pi \to +\infty.$$

The slope of U is given by

$$U'(\pi) = (1 - \alpha) + \alpha \, f'(\pi)$$

which is > 0 for $\alpha < 1/(1 + a)$ and < 0 for $\alpha > 1$.

The turning points of U are the roots of

$$f'(\pi) = 1 - 1/\alpha ,$$

which has two roots u_1, u_2 when

$$1/(1 + a) < \alpha < 1$$

and none otherwise.

By considering a sketch of $f'(\pi)$ it is a simple matter to see that

$$u_1 < v_1 \quad \text{and} \quad v_2 < u_2 .$$

Appendix 7.5

Because of the different shapes of the functions V and U over different parameter ranges the construction of F falls into a number of subcases, which we consider in turn.

(i) $\underline{\alpha \leq 1/(1 + a)}$

Differentiating equation (7.31) implicitly we find that

$$\frac{d\pi_{t+1}}{d\pi_t} = \frac{U'(\pi_t)}{V'(\pi_{t+1})} > 0,$$

for the set of α under consideration.

Note further that

$$\left. \frac{d\pi_{t+1}}{d\pi_t} \right)_{\pi_t=0} = \frac{1 - \alpha(1 + a)}{1 - \alpha a} < 1 .$$

By considering the limiting forms of V and U as $\pi \to \pm \infty$ we find that

$$\pi_{t+1} \sim (1 - \alpha)(\pi_t - f_\ell) \quad \text{as} \quad \pi_t \to +\infty,$$

and

$$\pi_{t+1} \sim (1 - \alpha)(\pi_t - f_u) \quad \text{as} \quad \pi_t \to -\infty.$$

Since $U' \neq 0$ in the case being considered, F must have the general shape shown in figure 7.11a.

(ii) $\underline{1/(1 + a) \leq \alpha \leq 1/a}$

For this set of α, U' is zero at u_1 and u_2 and hence F has turning points.

Specifically

$$\frac{d\pi_{t+1}}{d\pi_t} > 0 \qquad \text{for } u < u_1 \text{ and } u > u_2,$$

and

$$\frac{d\pi_{t+1}}{d\pi_t} \leq 0 \qquad \text{for } u_1 \leq u \leq u_2 .$$

The asymptotic form for F obtained in the previous subcase is still valid. We thus obtain figure 7.11b.

(iii) $\underline{1/a < \alpha < 1}$

For this set of α, U' = 0 at u_1, u_2 and V' = 0 at v_1, v_2. Recall that $v_1 > u_1$ and $v_2 < u_2$. Since the calculation of the slope of F requires U' at π_t and V' at π_{t+1} it is advisable to sketch on the same axes the graphs of U and V and using the relationship $V(\pi_{t+1}) = U(\pi_t)$ to determine the π_{t+1} corresponding to a given π_t. When this is done we find that

$$\frac{d\pi_{t+1}}{d\pi_t} \begin{cases} > 0 , & \text{for } u < u_1 \text{ and } u > u_2 , \\ \leq 0 , & \text{for } u_1 \leq u < u_1^* \text{ and } u_2^* < u \leq u_2, \\ > 0 , & \text{for } u_1^* < u < u_2, \\ \text{undefined}, & \text{for } u = u_1^* \text{ and } u = u_2^*. \end{cases}$$

We thus obtain figure 7.11c.

Here $u_1^* = U^{-1}(V(v_1))$ and $u_2^* = U^{-1}(V(v_2))$.

(iv) $\underline{\alpha \geq 1}$

For this set of α, U' < 0 for all u and V' = 0 at v_1, v_2. Using $V(\pi_{t+1}) = U(\pi_t)$ to determine the π_{t+1} corresponding to a given π_t we find that

$$\frac{d\pi_{t+1}}{d\pi_t} \begin{cases} > 0 , & \text{for } u < u_1^* \text{ and } u > u_2 , \\ > 0 , & \text{for } u_1^* < u , u_2^* , \\ \text{undefined}, & \text{for } u = u_1^* \text{ and } u = u_2^*. \end{cases}$$

We thus obtain figure 7.11d.

<u>**Appendix 7.6**</u>

Consider the differential equation model (7.16) which under perfect foresight ($\tau = 0$) becomes

$$\pi/\beta + f(\pi) + Y = 0, \tag{A1}$$

and

$$\dot{Y} = \pi. \tag{A2}$$

We have set $\mu = 0$ since we consider the case of constant money supply in the discrete time model.

We discretize the differential equation (A2) according to the scheme

$$Y_{t+1} - Y_t = \pi_t. \tag{A3}$$

By considering (A1) at $(t + 1)$ and t and subtracting we obtain

$$(\pi_{t+1} - \pi_t)/\beta + f(\pi_{t+1}) - f(\pi_t) + Y_{t+1} - Y_t = 0. \tag{A4}$$

Using (A3), replacing β by α and rearranging we obtain

$$\pi_{t+1} + \alpha f(\pi_{t+1}) = (1 - \alpha) \pi_t + \alpha f(\pi_t)$$

which is the difference equation (7.28).

The multivaluedness of the map F arises when the functions V and U both have turning points, as depicted in figure 7A3.

By choosing π^*_1 as the solution to $V(\pi) = U(\pi^*)$ (rather than the other two possible solutions) and π_1^{**} as the solution to $V(\pi) = U(\pi^{**})$ (rather than the other two possible solutions) the discrete map will impart to π_t the same basic dynamic behaviour as we observe in the limiting limit cycle of the continuous time model.   In this way we have arrived at the maps in figures 7.11(c) and (d).

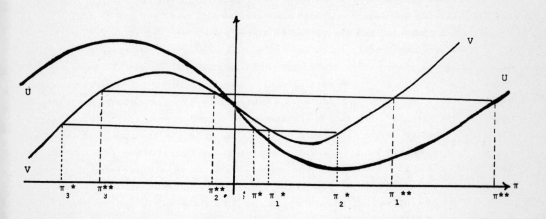

Figure 7A3

In chapter one we stated that the main aim of our thesis was to routinize the use of nonlinear methods in dynamic economic analysis. We achieved this aim by making use of the method of averaging and the method of discontinuous or relaxation oscillations to investigate nonlinear models which can be reduced to a set of nonlinear differential equations on the plane having limit cycle solutions. Higher dimensional models may be investigated by use of the concepts of centre manifold theory, which concentrates attention on limit cycle motion on an appropriate two dimensional manifold. The method of averaging usually yields a differential equation containing two elements. The first consists of the linearised part considered in the traditional local linear analysis. The second is a term which captures the qualitative effects of the nonlinearities in the model. The equilibrium of this differential equation approximates the amplitude of the limit cycle motion of the nonlinear model; by considering the effect of parameter shifts on this equilibrium we are able to determine the qualitative effects of parameter shifts on the amplitude of the cycle. In effect the qualitative analysis of the limit cycle equilibrium has been reduced to a comparative static type calculation since the principal achievement of the method of averaging is to reduce the analysis of a two dimensional limit cycle to that of a point equilibrium. The possibility of doing a comparative dynamic analysis in this way is an advantage of the approach we propose compared to those approaches referred to earlier in the thesis which rely on the use of existence theory of nonlinear differential equations and which cannot do much more than tell us that a limit cycle exists. One of the major criticisms of the use of limit cycles to model economic fluctuations is that the fluctuations are too regular but the discovery of the concept of chaotic behaviour overcomes this criticism - as we have seen such behaviour can arise in one dimensional difference equation models or in differential equation models of order at least three. We believe that the tools we have provided should allow the economic theorist to finally break free of the straitjacket of local linear analysis which has prevented a proper analysis of many important issues in dynamic economic theory. The economic theorist will henceforth be able to concentrate on questions such as when is a nonlinear analysis required, what are the important nonlinearities and how best to model these.

One such important issue is the theory of endogenous business cycles. In chapters three and four we used the nonlinear framework to analyse a number of endogenous business cycle theories. These were of the multiplier-accelerator type with and without the incorporation of the government budget restraint. We have barely scratched the surface of this important topic, however the framework we have set up can be used to undertake a systematic analysis of other major factors in the generation and propagation of business cycles such as wage and price dynamics, capital accumulation, costs and profits and uncertain expctations - all factors identified by Zarnowitz (1985) as being important elements in a theory of self-sustaining economic cycles. Some of these extensions will no doubt reduce to nonlinear differential equations on a two-dimensional manifold, either directly or via an application of centre manifold theory. Others are likely to exhibit their oscillatory motion via chaotic behaviour and will require an analysis parallelling that of the Lorenz equations in Sparrow(1983). The set of topics just listed may also require some technical extensions of the methods we are espousing. In particular we would like to be able to extend the method of averaging to handle time lags and stochastic elements. Practical methods for applying the method of averaging to nonlinear models involving time lags are discussed by Migulin et al (1983) ; using these methods it would be possible to incorporate for instance Kalecki's gestation period of investment into any of the nonlinear business cycle models we have discussed. Kalecki's (1935) discussion was in a linear framework and reveals that local instability is a possibility so a nonlinear analysis would seem appropriate. As far as the incorporation of stochastic elements is concerned a literature is emerging which enables the method of averaging in particular and bifurcation techniques in general to be applied to nonlinear systems containing random elements; we refer to Clarkson (1978), Watson and Reiss (1982) and Schuster (1984). The use of such techniques would be one approach to an analysis of uncertain expectations.

Many writers, in particular Zarnowitz (1985), Mullineux (1984) and Minsky(1982), have commented on the dichotomy in business cycle theory between real and monetary explanations. The multiplier accelerator models we have discussed concentrate on the real sector, however Hicks (1974) himself has stressed the need for a greater reliance on monetary factors. The search for monetary explanations led to the monetarist counter revolution in the 1950's and 1960's and a line of research which has culminated in the adjustment to random policy shock theories of Lucas (1975) and his followers. Zarnowitz enunciates a number of reasons why total reliance on such theories is unsatisfactory and sees a need for a synthesis of real and monetary theories. It is our belief that one approach to such a synthesis could be via the use of the dynamic theory of weakly interconnected nonlinear systems as discussed in Evans and Fradellos (1982) and Singh (1985). These ideas would allow a qualitative analysis of a four dimensional nonlinear differential system which is what a proper synthesis would lead to - two differential equations for the dynamics of each sector. Such an approach would, for instance, allow an elaboration of Minsky's (1957) theories incorporating monetary factors into multiplier-accelerator models. It is likely that this line of approach could yield that model, or rather class of models, towards which business cycle theorists have neen groping since the years of high theory; namely models large enough to capture the essential features of the real and financial sectors but small enough to allow a qualitative analysis of the effects of policy and exogenous parameter shifts. This path should also enable economic theorists to undertake the task of comparing within a unified framework the main business cycle theories of the interwar years to which we alluded in chapter one. The recent study by Hansonn (1982) which views the dynamic method of the Stockholm school of that era from a modern perspective indictes the timeliness of such a task.

Our view on the dynamic instability problem (chapter seven) may be extended in a number of ways. To the continuous time model we could add a third differential equation to cater for capital accumulation. We would then be analysing the so-called generalised Tobin model for which Benhabib and Miyao (1981) have performed a local linear analysis and applied the Hopf bifurcation theorem to demonstrate the existence of limit cycle motion in this three-dimensional system. Their analysis may be carried further by including a nonlinearity of the type we introduced in chapter seven and applying centre-manifold theory; it is highly likely that this model would exhibit chaotic behaviour via the period doubling route. Our discrete time analysis in chapter seven considered only the perfect foresight case. It would be of interest to also analyse the dynamics of the adaptive expectations case, which can be expressed as a nonlinear system of two difference equations and is likely to yield strange attractor behaviour. Our discrete time analysis has considered a deterministic, nonlinear version of the stochastic, linear model investigated by Burmeister (1980a); it would be of interest to complete this analysis by considering a stochastic, nonlinear model. For this task the approach to nonlinear stochastic models suggested by Samuelson (1947) could be a fruitful one.

Many areas of economic theory may benefit from a nonlinear dynamic analysis. We have already spoken at length about business cycle theory. All those models which exhibit the behaviour characteristic of the dynamic instability problem are clearly in need of an analysis from the nonlinear viewpoint, the main task being to identify and model the important nonlinearities. Models of exchange rate dynamics seem ready for such an approach; Gray and Turnovsky (1979) demonstrated dynamic instability behaviour in a class of such models - nonlinear versions of these would be formally equivalent to the generalised Tobin model referred to in the previous paragraph.

Another area which could possibly benefit from the nonlinear viewpoint is the issue of market efficiency. The efficient market hypothesis has undergone a number of empirical tests, see Sheffrin (1983), but Shiller (1981) has shown that simple efficient market models are not adequately able to explain the variance of stock prices. Most of these models are based on discrete linear dynamics and it is tempting to speculate that nonlinear versions of these models would yield chaotic behaviour, which to the observer appears random. Such models could reconcile the viewpoint that in financial markets agents do make use of past price data with the view that price movements in such markets are completely random. A possible starting point of such an analysis would be to apply to financial data the empirical tests of chaotic behaviour discussed by Schuster (1985).

It is clear that the use of a systematic framework for nonlinear dynamics is going to open new vistas for the economic theorist. Old problems may be approached from a new perspective and new problems may be tackled. Ichimura (1955) entitled his article, surveying the nonlinear methods available at his time of writing, "Towards a general nonlinear macrodynamic theory of economic fluctuations". All the elements of such a general theory are now at hand and the task of constructing it should prove rewarding and exciting.

REFERENCES

Abraham, R.H. and Shaw, C.P. (1984), **Dynamics - The Geometry of Behaviour**, Aerial Press Inc., Santa Cruz, California,

Allais, M. (1956), "Explication des cycles economiques par un modele non lineaire a regulation retardee", Metroeconomica, $\underline{8}$, 4-83.

Allen, R.G.D. (1967), **Macro-Economic Theory: A Mathematical Treatment**, MacMillan, London.

Andronov, A.M., Vitt, A.A. and Chaikin, S.E. (1966), **Theory of Oscillators**, Pergamon, London.

Arnold, V.I. (1973), **Ordinary Differential Equations**, M.I.T. Press, Cambridge, MA. (Russian original, Moscow 1971).

Benhabib, J. and Day R.H. (1982), "A Characterization of Erratic Dynamics in the Overlapping Generations Model", Journal of Economic Dynamics and Control, $\underline{4}$, 37-55.

Benhabib, J. and Miyao, T.(1981), "New Results on the Dynamics of the Generalised Tobin Model", International Economic Review, $\underline{22}$, 589 - 596.

Black, F (1974) "Uniqueness of the price level in monetary growth models with rational expectations", Journal of Economic Theory $\underline{7}$, 53-65.

Blanchard, O.J. (1979) "Backward and forward solutions for economies with rational expectations", American Economic Review, $\underline{69}$, 114-118.

Blanchard, O.J. (1981) "Output, the Stock Market and Interest Rates", American Economic Review, $\underline{71}$, 132-143.

Blatt, J.M. (1978), "On the Econometric Approach to Business Cycle Analysis", Oxford Economic Papers, 30 (2), 292-300.

Blatt, J.M. (1980), "On the Frisch Model of Business Cycles", Oxford Economic Papers, 32, 467-479.

Blatt, J.M. (1983), **Dynamic Economic Systems: A Post-Keynesian Approach**, Wheatsheaf Books, Brighton, England.

Blinder, A.S. and Solow, R.M. (1973), "Does Fiscal Policy Matter?", Journal of Public Economics, 2, 319-337.

Bothwell, F.E. (1952), "The Method of Equivalent Linearization", Econometrica, 20, 269-283.

Bray, M.M. (1983), "Convergence to Rational Expectations Equilibrium", in R. Frydman and E.S. Phelps (eds.) **Individual Forecasting and Aggregate Outcomes**, Cambridge University Press.

Brock, W.A. (1975), "A Simple Perfect Foresight Monetary Model", Journal of Monetary Economics, 1, 133-150.

Burmeister, E. (1980a), **Capital Theory and Dynamics**, Cambridge Univeristy Press.

Burmeister, E. (1980b) "On Some conceptual issues in rational expectations modelling", Journal of Money, Credit and Banking, 12, 800-816.

Cagan, P. (1956), "The Monetary Dynamics of Hyperinflation", in **Studies in the Quantity Theory of Money**, (M. Friedman,ed.), University of Chicago Press, Chicago.

Calvo, G. (1977), "The Stability of Models of Money and Perfect Foresight: A Comment", Econometrica, 45, 1737-1739.

Carlson, J.A. (1968), "An Invariably Stable Cobweb Model", Review of Economic Studies, 35, 360-362.

Chang, W.W. and Smyth, D.J. (1971), "The existence and persistence of cycles in a nonlinear model: Kaldor's 1940 model re-examined", Review of Economic Studies, 38, 37-44.

Chillingworth, D.R.J. (1976), **Differentiable Topology with a View to Applications**, Pitman, London.

Christ, C.F. (1968), "A Simple Macroeconomic Model with a Government Budget Restraint", Journal of Political Economy, 76, 53-67.

Clarkson, B.L. (1978), **Stochastic Problems in Dynamics**, Pitman, London.

Day, R.H. (1982), "Irregular Growth Cycles", American Economic Review, 72, 406-414.

Desai, M. (1973), "Growth Cycles and Inflation in a Model of Class Struggle", Journal of Economic Theory, 6, 527-545.

Ezekiel, M. (1938), "The Cobweb Theorem", Quarterly Journal of Economics, 52, 255-280.

Evans, F.J. and Fradellos, G. (1982), "The Qualitative Analysis of Nonlinear Dynamic Economic Systems by Structural Methods", in G. Szego (ed.) **New Quantitative Techniques for Economic Analysis**, Academic Press.

Evans, J.L. and Yarrow G.K. (1981), "Some implications of Alternative Expectations Hypotheses in the Monetary Analysis of Hyperinflation", Oxford Economic Papers 34, 61-80.

Feigenbaum, M.J. (1983), "Universal Behaviour in Nonlinear Systems", Essay No. 7 in **Nonlinear Dynamics and Turbulence**, ed. G.I. Ioos, Pitman.

Ferri, P. and Greenberg, E. (1989), **The Labour Market and Business Cycle Theories**, Springer-Verlag Lecture Notes in Economics and Mathematical Systems, Vol 325.

Freedman, H.I. and Waltman, P. (1975), "Perturbation of Two-Dimensional Predator-Prey Equations", SIAM Journal of Applied Mathematics, 28, 1-10.

Frisch, R. (1933), "Propogation Problems and Impulse Problems in Dynamic Economics", in **Essays in Honour of Gustav Cassell**, Allen and Unwin, London.

Gabisch, G. and Lorenz, H.W. (1989), **Business Cycle Theory: A Survey of Methods and Concepts**, Springer-Verlag Universitext.

Gandolfo, G. (1980), **Economic Dynamics: Methods and Models**, North Holland, Amsterdam.

Goldman, S. (1972), "Hyperinflation and the Rate of Growth in the Money Supply", Journal of Economic Theory, 5, 250-257.

Goodwin, R.M. (1950), "A Nonlinear Theory of the Cycle", Review of Economic Statistics, XXXII, 4, 316-320.

Goodwin, R.M. (1951), "The Nonlinear Accelerator and the Persistence of Business Cycles", Econometrica, 19, No. 1, January, 1-17.

Goodwin, R.M. (1967), "A Growth Cycle", in C.H. Feinstein (ed.), **Socialism, Capitalism and Growth**, C.U.P., Cambridge.

Goodwin, R.M., Krieger, M. and Vercelli, A. (1984), (eds.) **Nonlinear Models of Fluctuating Growth**, Springer-Verlag.

Gray, M. and Turnovsky, S.J. (1979), "The Stability of Exchange Rate Dynamics Under Perfect Myopic Foresight", International Economic Review, 20, 643-660.

Guckenheimer, J. and Holmes, P. (1983), **Nonlinear Oscillations, Dynamical Systems and Bifurcations of Vector Fields**, Springer-Verlag, New York.

Guckenheimer, J. (1984) Review of "The Lorenz Equations: Bifurcations, Chaos and Strange Attractors" by C Sparrow, Springer-Verlag 1982. American Mathematical Monthly, May 1984, 325-6.

Hadjimichalakis, M.G. (1971), "Equilibrium and Disequilibrium Growth with Money - The Tobin Models", Review of Economic Studies, 38, 457-479.

Hadjimichalakis, M.G. (1981), "Expectation of the 'myopic perfect foresight' variety in monetary dynamics", Journal of Economic Dynamics and Control, 3, 157-176.

Hahn, F.H. (1960) "The Stability of Growth Equilibrium", Quarterly Journal of Economics, 74, 206-226.

Hahn, F.H. (1966) "Equilibrium Dynamics with Heterogeneous Capital Goods", Quarterly Journal of Economics, 80, 633-646.

Hansson, B.A. (1982), **The Stockholm School and the Development of Dynamic Method**, Croom-Helm, 1982.

Hartman, P. and Olech, C. (1962), "On Global Asymptotic Stability of Solutions of Ordinary Differential Equations", Transactions of the American Mathematical Society, 104, 154-178.

Hickman B.G., (ed) (1972), **Econometric Models of Cyclical Behaviour**, vols.1 and 2 NBER Studies in Income and Wealth No. 3V, Princeton University Press.

Hicks, J.R. (1950), **A Contribution to the Theory of the Trade Cycle**, Oxford, Clarendon.

Hicks, J.R. (1974), "Real and Monetary Factors in Economic Fluctuations", Scottish Journal of Political Economy, 21, 205-214.

Hirsch, M.W. and Smale, S. (1974), **Differential Equations, Dynamical Systems and Linear Algebra**, Academic Press, N.Y.

Ichimura, S. (1955), "Towards a General Nonlinear Macrodynamic Theory of Economic Fluctuations", Ch. 8 in K. Kurihari (ed.), **Post Keynesian Economics**, New Jersey : Rutgers University Press.

Infante, E.F. and Stein, J.L. (1980), "Money Financed Fiscal Policy in a Growing Economy", Journal of Political Economy, 88, 259-287.

Jensen, R.V. and Urban, R. (1984), "Chaotic Behaviour in a Non-linear Cobweb Model", Economics Letters, 15, 235-240.

Kaldor, N. (1940), "A Model of the Trade Cycle", Economic Journal, 50, 78-92.

Kaldor, N. (1972), "The Irrelevance of Equilibrium Economics", Economic Journal, 82, 1237-1255.

Kalecki, M. (1935), "A Macrodynamic Theory of Business Cycles", Econometrica, 3, 327-344.

Kemp, M.C. and Kimura, Y. (1978), **Introduction to Mathematical Economics**, Springer-Verlag, N.Y.

Keynes, J.M. (1936), **The General Theory of Employment, Interest and Money**, Harcourt, Brace and World, New York.

Kolmogoroff, A. (1978), "Sulla Teoria di Volterra della Lotta per l'Esistenza", Giorn. Ist. Ital. Attuari, 7, 74-80, 1936. Reprinted and translated in Scudo, F. (ed.) **The Golden Age of Theoretical Ecology**, Springer-Verlag, New York.

Kregel, J.A. (1980), "The Theoretical Consequences of Economic Methodology: Samuelson's Foundations", Metroeconomica, XXXII, 1, 25-38.

Krylov, N.M., and Bogoliubov, N.N. (1947), **Introduction to Nonlinear Mechanics**, Princeton University Press. Russian Original, Moscow, 1937.

La Salle, J. (1949), "Relaxation Oscillations", Quarterly of Applied Mathematics, 7, 1-19

Leontief, W.W. (1934), "Verzogerte Angebotsanpassing und Partielles Gleichgewicht", Zeitschrift fur Nationalokonomie, V, bd. 5, 670-676.

Levinson, N. and Smith, O.K. (1942), "A General Equation for Relaxation Oscillations", Duke Math. J., 9, 382-403.

Li, T.I. and Yorke, A.J. (1975), "Period Three Implies Chaos", American Mathematical Monthly, 82, 985-992.

Lichtenberg, A.J. and Lieberman, M.A. (1983) "Regular and Stochastic Motion", Springer-Verlag, N.Y.

Liénard, A. (1928), "Etude des Oscillations Entretenues", Revue Générale de l'Electricité, 23, 901-946.

Lorenz, E.N. (1963), "Deterministic Non-periodic Flows", Journal of Atmospheric Science, 20, 130-141.

Lorenz, H.W. (1989), **Nonlinear Dynamical Economics and Chaotic Motion**, Springer-Verlag Lecture Notes in Economics and Mathematical Systems, Vol. 334.

Lucas, R.E. Jr. (1975), "An Equilibrium Model of the Business Cycle", Journal of Political Economy, 83, 1113-1144.

Manning, R. (1970), "Stability of Cobwebs", Economic Record, 46 , 588-589.

Manning, R. (1971), "A Generalization of a Cobweb Theorem", Review of Economic Studies, 38, 123-125.

Markus, L. (1971), **Lectures in Differentiable Dynamics**. A.M.S. Publications: Providence.

Marsden, J.E. and McCracken, M.F. (1976), **The Hopf Bifurcation and its Application** Applied Math. Sciences, Vol. 19, Springer-Verlag, Berlin.

May, R.M. (1976a), "Simple Mathematical Models with Very Complicated Dynamics", Nature, 261, 459-467.

May, R.M. (1976b), **Theoretical Ecology: Principles and Applications**, Blackwell Scientific, Oxford.

May, R.M. (1983), "Nonlinear Problems in Ecology and Resource Management", in G. Iooss (ed.) **Chaotic Behaviour of Deterministic Systems**, North-Holland.

McCallum, B.T. (1983), "On Non-uniqueness in Rational Expectations Models", Journal of Monetary Economics 11, 139-168.

Meadows, D.L. (1970), **Dynamics of Commodity Production Cycles**, Wright-Allen Press, Cambridge, Mass.

Medio, A.(1979), **Teoria Nonlineare del Ciclo Economico**, Società Editrice il Mulino, Bologna.

Meyer, W.J.(1984), **Concepts of Mathematical Modelling**, McGraw-Hill, New York

Migulin, V., Medvedev, V., Mustel, E. and Parygin, V. (1983), **Basic Theory of Oscillations**, Mir, Moscow.

Minorsky, N. (1962), **Nonlinear Oscillaltions**, Van Nostrand, New York.

Minsky, H.P. (1957), "Monetary Systems and Accelerator Models", American Economic Review, $\underline{47}$, 859-883.

Minsky, H.P. (1982), **Inflation, Recession and Economic Policy**, Wheatsheaf Books, Brighton, England.

Mullineux, A.W. (1984), **The Business Cycle after Keynes**, Wheatsheaf Books, Brighton.

Nerlove, M. (1958), "Adaptive Expectations and Cobweb Phenomena", Quarterly Journal of Economics, $\underline{72}$, 227-240.

Obstfeld, M. and Rogoff, K. (1983), "Speculative Hyperinflations in Maximizing Models: Can we Rule them Out?", Journal of Political Economy, $\underline{91}$, 675-687.

Olech, C. (1963), "On the Global Stability of an Autonomous System on the Plane" in **Contributions to Differential Equations**, (J.P. La Salle ed.) vol. 1, Interscience New York.

Orsag, S.A. and McLaughlin, J.B. (1980), "Evidence that Random Behaviour is Generic for Nonlinear Differential Equations", Physica 1D, 68-79.

Oster, G. (1978), "The Dynamics of Nonlinear Models with Age Structure", in **Studies in Mathematical Biology**, Pt II, Math. Assoc. America, Washington.

Peixoto, M.M. (1962), "Structural Stability on Two-dimensional Manifolds", Topology, $\underline{1}$, 101-120.

Ploeg, F. (1983), "Economic Growth and Conflict over the Distribution of Income", Journal of Economic Dynamics and Control, $\underline{6}$, 253-279.

Rau, N. (1985), "Simplifying the Theory of the Government Budget Restraint", Oxford Economic Papers, 37, 210-229.

Rayleigh, R. (1877), **The Theory of Sound**, Dover Edition 1945, New York.

Rose, H. (1967), "On the Nonlinear Theory of the Employment cycle", Review of Economic Studies, 34, 138-152.

Rossler, O.E. (1979), "Continuous Chaos - Four Prototype Equations", Annals of New York Academy of Sciences, 376-392.

Samuelson, P.A. (1947) **Foundations of Economic Analysis**, Harvard University Press, Cambridge, Mass.

Samuelson, P.A. (1967) "Indeterminacy of Development in a Heterogeneous-Capital Model with Constant Saving Propensity". In **Essays on the Theory of Optimal Economic Growth**, ed. K Shell, M.I.T. Press, Cambridge, Mass.

Sargent, T.J. and Wallace, N. (1973), "The Stability of Models of Money and Growth with Perfect Foresight", Econometrica, 41, 1043-1048.

Scarth, W.M. (1985) "A Note on Non-uniqueness in Rational Expectations Models", Journal of Monetary Economics 15, 247-254.

Schinasi, G.J. (1981), "A Nonlinear Dynamic Model of Short Run Fluctuations", Review of Economic Studies, XLVIII, 649-656.

Schinasi, G.J. (1982), "Fluctuations in a Dynamic, Intermediate-run IS-LM Model: Applications of the Poincare-Bendixsen Theorem", Journal of Economic Theory, 28, 369-375.

Schuster, H.G. (1985), "Deterministic Chaos", Physic-Verlag, Weinheim.

Sheffrin, S.M. (1983), "Rational Expectations", Cambridge University Press.

Shiller, R.J. (1978), "Rational Expectations and the Dynamic Structure of Macroeconomic Models: A Critical Review", Journal of Monetary Economics ,4, 1-44.

Singh, Y.P. (1985), "Stability Analysis of Weakly Interconnected Nonlinear Systems", International Journal of Systems Science, 16, 713-725.

Sims, C.A. (ed.) (1977), **New Methods in Business Cycle Research**, Federal Reserve Bank of Minneopolis.

Smale, S. (1963), "Diffeomorphisms with many periodic points", in **Differential and Combinatorial Topology**, S.S. Cairns (ed.), Princeton University Press, Princeton.

Sparrow, C. (1983), **The Lorenz Equations: Birfurcations, Chaos and Strange Attractors**, Springer-Verlag, Berlin.

Stoker, J. (1950), **Nonlinear Vibrations**, Interscience Publishers, New York.

Taylor, J.B. (1977), "Conditions for Unique Solutions in Stochastic Macro-economic Models with Rational Expectations", Econometrica, 45, 1377-1385.

Tobin, J. (1965), "Money and Economic Growth", Econometrica, 33, 671-684.

Torre, V. (1977), "The existence of limit cycles and control in complete Keynesian systems by theory of bifurcations", Econometrica, 45, 1457-1466.

Turnovsky, S.J. (1977), **Macroeconomic Analysis and Stabilization Policy**, Cambridge University Press.

Velupillai, K. (1979), "Some Stability Properties of Goodwin's Growth cycle", Z. fur Nationalokonomie, 39, 245-257.

Volterra, V. (1931), **Theorie Mathematique de la Lutte pour la Vie**, Gauthier-Villars, Paris.

Watson, J.G. and Reiss, E.L. (1982), "A Statistical Theory for Imperfect Bifurcation", SIAM Journal of Applied Mathematics, 42, 135-14.

Zarnowitz, V. (1985), "Business Cycle Theory", Journal of Economic Literature, 23, 523-580.

Vol. 292: I. Tchijov, L. Tomaszewicz (Eds.), Input-Output Modeling. Proceedings, 1985. VI, 195 pages. 1987.

Vol. 293: D. Batten, J. Casti, B. Johansson (Eds.), Economic Evolution and Structural Adjustment. Proceedings, 1985. VI, 382 pages. 1987.

Vol. 294: J. Jahn, W. Krabs (Eds.), Recent Advances and Historical Development of Vector Optimization. VII, 405 pages. 1987.

Vol. 295: H. Meister, The Purification Problem for Constrained Games with Incomplete Information. X, 127 pages. 1987.

Vol. 296: A. Börsch-Supan, Econometric Analysis of Discrete Choice. VIII, 211 pages. 1987.

Vol. 297: V. Fedorov, H. Läuter (Eds.), Model-Oriented Data Analysis. Proceedings, 1987. VI, 239 pages. 1988.

Vol. 298: S.H. Chew, Q. Zheng, Integral Global Optimization. VII, 179 pages. 1988.

Vol. 299: K. Marti, Descent Directions and Efficient Solutions in Discretely Distributed Stochastic Programs. XIV, 178 pages. 1988.

Vol. 300: U. Derigs, Programming in Networks and Graphs. XI, 315 pages. 1988.

Vol. 301: J. Kacprzyk, M. Roubens (Eds.), Non-Conventional Preference Relations in Decision Making. VII, 155 pages. 1988.

Vol. 302: H.A. Eiselt, G. Pederzoli (Eds.), Advances in Optimization and Control. Proceedings, 1986. VIII, 372 pages. 1988.

Vol. 303: F.X. Diebold, Empirical Modeling of Exchange Rate Dynamics. VII, 143 pages. 1988.

Vol. 304: A. Kurzhanski, K. Neumann, D. Pallaschke (Eds.), Optimization, Parallel Processing and Applications. Proceedings, 1987. VI, 292 pages. 1988.

Vol. 305: G.-J.C.Th. van Schijndel, Dynamic Firm and Investor Behaviour under Progressive Personal Taxation. X, 215 pages. 1988.

Vol. 306: Ch. Klein, A Static Microeconomic Model of Pure Competition. VIII, 139 pages. 1988.

Vol. 307: T.K. Dijkstra (Ed.), On Model Uncertainty and its Statistical Implications. VII, 138 pages. 1988.

Vol. 308: J.R. Daduna, A. Wren (Eds.), Computer-Aided Transit Scheduling. VIII, 339 pages. 1988.

Vol. 309: G. Ricci, K. Velupillai (Eds.), Growth Cycles and Multisectoral Economics: the Goodwin Tradition. III, 126 pages. 1988.

Vol. 310: J. Kacprzyk, M. Fedrizzi (Eds.), Combining Fuzzy Imprecision with Probabilistic Uncertainty in Decision Making. IX, 399 pages. 1988.

Vol. 311: R. Färe, Fundamentals of Production Theory. IX, 163 pages. 1988.

Vol. 312: J. Krishnakumar, Estimation of Simultaneous Equation Models with Error Components Structure. X, 357 pages. 1988.

Vol. 313: W. Jammernegg, Sequential Binary Investment Decisions. VI, 156 pages. 1988.

Vol. 314: R. Tietz, W. Albers, R. Selten (Eds.), Bounded Rational Behavior in Experimental Games and Markets. VI, 368 pages. 1988.

Vol. 315: I. Orishimo, G.J.D. Hewings, P. Nijkamp (Eds.), Information Technology: Social and Spatial Perspectives. Proceedings, 1986. VI, 268 pages. 1988.

Vol. 316: R.L. Basmann, D.J. Slottje, K. Hayes, J.D. Johnson, D.J. Molina, The Generalized Fechner-Thurstone Direct Utility Function and Some of its Uses. VIII, 159 pages. 1988.

Vol. 317: L. Bianco, A. La Bella (Eds.), Freight Transport Planning and Logistics. Proceedings, 1987. X, 568 pages. 1988.

Vol. 318: T. Doup, Simplicial Algorithms on the Simplotope. VIII, 262 pages. 1988.

Vol. 319: D.T. Luc, Theory of Vector Optimization. VIII, 173 pages. 1989.

Vol. 320: D. van der Wijst, Financial Structure in Small Business. VII, 181 pages. 1989.

Vol. 321: M. Di Matteo, R.M. Goodwin, A. Vercelli (Eds.), Technological and Social Factors in Long Term Fluctuations. Proceedings. IX, 442 pages. 1989.

Vol. 322: T. Kollintzas (Ed.), The Rational Expectations Equilibrium Inventory Model. XI, 269 pages. 1989.

Vol. 323: M.B.M. de Koster, Capacity Oriented Analysis and Design of Production Systems. XII, 245 pages. 1989.

Vol. 324: I.M. Bomze, B.M. Pötscher, Game Theoretical Foundations of Evolutionary Stability. VI, 145 pages. 1989.

Vol. 325: P. Ferri, E. Greenberg, The Labor Market and Business Cycle Theories. X, 183 pages. 1989.

Vol. 326: Ch. Sauer, Alternative Theories of Output, Unemployment, and Inflation in Germany: 1960–1985. XIII, 206 pages. 1989.

Vol. 327: M. Tawada, Production Structure and International Trade. V, 132 pages. 1989.

Vol. 328: W. Güth, B. Kalkofen, Unique Solutions for Strategic Games. VII, 200 pages. 1989.

Vol. 329: G. Tillmann, Equity, Incentives, and Taxation. VI, 132 pages. 1989.

Vol. 330: P.M. Kort, Optimal Dynamic Investment Policies of a Value Maximizing Firm. VII, 185 pages. 1989.

Vol. 331: A. Lewandowski, A.P. Wierzbicki (Eds.), Aspiration Based Decision Support Systems. X, 400 pages. 1989.

Vol. 332: T.R. Gulledge, Jr., L.A. Litteral (Eds.), Cost Analysis Applications of Economics and Operations Research. Proceedings. VII, 422 pages. 1989.

Vol. 333: N. Dellaert, Production to Order. VII, 158 pages. 1989.

Vol. 334: H.-W. Lorenz, Nonlinear Dynamical Economics and Chaotic Motion. XI, 248 pages. 1989.

Vol. 335: A.G. Lockett, G. Islei (Eds.), Improving Decision Making in Organisations. Proceedings. IX, 606 pages. 1989.

Vol. 336: T. Puu, Nonlinear Economic Dynamics. VII, 119 pages. 1989.

Vol. 337: A. Lewandowski, I. Stanchev (Eds.), Methodology and Software for Interactive Decision Support. VIII, 309 pages. 1989.

Vol. 338: J.K. Ho, R.P. Sundarraj, DECOMP: an Implementation of Dantzig-Wolfe Decomposition for Linear Programming. VI, 206 pages. 1989.

Vol. 339: J. Terceiro Lomba, Estimation of Dynamic Econometric Models with Errors in Variables. VIII, 116 pages. 1990.

Vol. 340: T. Vasko, R. Ayres, L. Fontvieille (Eds.), Life Cycles and Long Waves. XIV, 293 pages. 1990.

Vol. 341: G.R. Uhlich, Descriptive Theories of Bargaining. IX, 165 pages. 1990.

Vol. 342: K. Okuguchi, F. Szidarovszky, The Theory of Oligopoly With Multi-Product Firms. V, 167 pages. 1990.

Vol. 343: C. Chiarella, The Elements of a Nonlinear Theory of Economic Dynamics. IX, 149 pages. 1990.